# JOSEPH
## CEO & PRESIDENT

Not only a dreamer

Rivelino Montenegro, PhD

# Joseph, CEO & President
## Not only a Dreamer

Rivelino Montenegro, PhD

Cover and graphic design: José Roberto Rodrigues (www.roberttusdesign.com)

**Printed in Germany**

To order more copies of this book or a version in a different language visit:

# www.josephceo.com

# Index

# Preface

I always wanted to ride a roller coaster, but fear stopped me. Then a day I dared to do it. Ten seconds into the ride, I was promising myself I would never do it again. A few days later, there was I, screaming and promising the same.

Since I graduated from university I see no need of a roller coaster ride to feel an adrenaline rush. My professional life has been the biggest roller coaster I have ever faced, with crises after crises, ups, downs, full stops and some inevitable falls.

It is interesting however to look around and see that I am not alone in this ride.

In the economical crisis that started in 2007 in the US and quickly engulfed the whole world, it is estimated that 2.6 million people in the US lost their jobs in 2008. Although the crisis had its beginning in the American mortgage market, it hit the whole world, and in all areas, from automotive to pharmaceuticals. Stock market had major losses. Strong economies such as the American and Japanese fell into recession.

Fear spread all around and economists with all possible theories could not help to find a quick solution. Economist Paul Krugman, Nobel Prize winner, argued that much of the past 30 years of macroeconomics was "spectacularly useless at best, and positively harmful at worst."[1]

The lesson is simple and hard: Crises are part of the game and you must be ready to face them.

You may not know, but most books on Economics define recession as a normal part (although unpleasing) of the economic cycle. Normal? Yes, normal! Crises come and go! The Economy grows for some time, falls, but grows again...

In fact, crises belong to larger tendencies and to a certain extent, predictable. Therefore, as in the case of some cyclical natural phenomena, crises are also known as examples of the "Joseph effect", after the biblical character Joseph of Egypt. Joseph was the one who interpreted the Pharaoh's dreams about the seven fat cows and seven meager ones. The two classes of cows represented seven years of plenty followed by seven years of famine (or recession), respectively.

This episode was probably the first one to use animals to represent the market tendency. The fat cows for a growing economy and the meager one for an economic recession. Nowadays the bull, which with braveness and hasty strikes is the symbol for optimism and commitment, while the bear on the other hand with a heavy gait represents difficulty and stagnation.

Joseph's story is the journey of a young man who arrived in Egypt as a slave, but overcame all difficulties to become the second most important person in the country,

---

[1] The Economist, July 18th 2009

similar to a prime minister of a nation or a CEO of a company. He came in play right in time to restructure a nation that in seven years would have to face one of the hardest crises that could hurt a country.

What made him the right person to lead Egypt? What skills did he have and what was his character like to enable him to overcome all prejudices and hurdles of that time to reach the top and to help to turn Egypt into the world's granary?

Betrayed by his own brothers, sold as a slave and finally imprisoned unjustly! What characteristics and skills were needed to overcome such situation, turn around, achieve the leadership and stay as a leader for years? As you will see in this book, it was neither enough to dream nor to interpret dreams.

If you think that all you need to win in life is to have a dream or vision, then wake up! Having a dream is just the first part. Dreams provide a good set of directions, but they do not guarantee victory.

If Joseph were just the dreamer that his brothers ironically called him of, he would never had achieved what he did.

This book analyses the essential characteristics that Joseph had, which are the same characteristics that anyone who wants to be a leader[2] in business or politics must develop. Thus the title: Joseph, CEO & President.

---

[2] The term "leader" in this book has a broad meaning. A leader here is more closely related to someone who becomes a positive example in his profession than to the leading person of a company or of a country.

Here you will also have the opportunity to get familiar with modern examples and to read interviews with people who experienced ups and downs in their professional lives. You will also see how the concepts and ideas that were important for Joseph many centuries ago are as important for us today.

Dreams can be different, but the requirements to turn them into reality are basically the same.

The ability to interpret dreams was a gift from God, the others skills Joseph possessed were developed, something that you can do to.

If you still have no dreams, maybe this is the time to start dreaming, but awaken! Then take the needed steps to achieve your dreams. The purpose of this book is to help you.

# Introduction

Joseph lived with his father, Jacob, and his brothers in Canaan, a region in the Middle East (the full story can be found in the book of Genesis, chapters 37 and 39 to 50).

Jacob, Joseph's father was very rich. The family administered a large estate, consisting of a great number of camels, cattle and donkeys.

The patriarch Jacob clearly showed his preference for Joseph. And against the tradition of that time, he intended to place Joseph as the leader of the family, although he was not the first-born. To show his decision, Jacob gave his young son a coat of many colors to distinguish him from his other sons. The old patriarch committed one of the biggest mistakes in both private and public administration: Choosing a successor (a leader) and expecting everyone to accept it, just because he was chosen by the "patriarch".
Leadership can not be given or imposed, it must be conquered!

Joseph was not yet ready to be the leader of the family. He had the potential, but had to gain experience to conquer that position.

Besides the coat, Joseph's dreams increased his brothers' envy, because in such dreams, he was always presented as the leader of the family.

The brothers' envy turned into hate and made them plot against Joseph's life. However, the oldest brother, moved by compassion and in consideration to his father, convinced them to give up the cruel idea of killing Joseph and to sell him instead. They sold him as a slave to a group of Ishmaelites that were passing through the region. The Ishmaelites took him to Egypt, where he was sold as a slave to an Egyptian official called Potiphar. This official meanwhile noticed Joseph's noble character as well as his administrative skills. Quickly, Joseph was promoted from simple slave to the butler of the official's house.

After some time, Potiphar's wife fell in love with Joseph and started to pursue him. But he firmly resisted, out of respect and consideration for the trust that Potiphar had put on him. One day, however, when Joseph came to work nobody was at home, except for Potiphar's wife. She tried to seduce him again, but this time with a more direct and aggressive approach, grabbing him by this clothes. Joseph resisted, but to flee he had to free himself from his own clothes. As a result of another unsuccessful attempt, the woman flew into rage, transforming her passion to hate. She told her husband that Joseph had tried to abuse her. The clothes were the proof and as consequence Joseph arrested.

The prison keeper also noticed Joseph's administrative skills. He used Joseph as a manager although he was a prisoner. Although in a miserable situation, Joseph had the opportunity to develop his skills and use his talents to help others.

After some time, two important servants of Pharaoh, the chief butler and the baker, were arrested into the prison which was being managed by Joseph. The chief butler was responsible for inspecting and tasting all drinks served to Pharaoh, while the baker dealt with the food. Pharaoh had probably suffered food poisoning, which could have been a plot from an enemy. Since it was not yet clear whether the poisoning from what he ate or drank, both servants were arrested until investigations could reveal who was accountable for the problem.

While in prison, both servants in the same night had dreams that disturbed them. Joseph offered to help interpret their dreams. Joseph told the chief butler that he would soon be free and return to his work. But the interpretation of the baker's dream was dreadful. In three days, he would be executed per Pharaoh's order.

After three days, Joseph's interpretation came true.

Some time later, Pharaoh had a disturbing dream. No official or anyone else in the kingdom could offer an interpretation of this dream. At that moment, the chief butler remembered Joseph and told Pharaoh about a young prisoner who was skilled in the art of dream interpretation. Pharaoh called Joseph. A great opportunity came through for Joseph. He finally had the possibility to show his talents before the greatest authority in all Egypt.

Joseph not only gave the interpretation of the dream, which showed that a time of economic crisis was approaching, but he also offered a plan to help solve the problem. His skills and intelligence impressed Pharaoh in such a way, that he decided to appoint the young Joseph as the second most important person in Egypt, similar to a CEO of a company, President, or Prime Minister of a country.

Joseph carried out this role for many years, helping to turn Egypt into a world granary, consolidating the Egyptian economy such that the nation could endure the approaching seven-year crisis.

At that time, the region where Joseph's family lived was devastated by drought. His brothers had to come to Egypt, where they could buy grains. Once in there, the brothers (the same who sold Joseph) did not recognize him, because they could not imagine finding him there, much less in such a high-ranking position. Joseph recognized them, but did not reveal himself. He then, through a series of tests discovered that his brothers had finally matured and left behind their violent and grudging nature.

Joseph finally revealed himself to his brothers and brought his whole family from the impoverished region to live in Egypt.

Due to Joseph's good reputation, Pharaoh gave Jacob's family land in the region of Goshen, where they established their residency.

Once again Joseph lived up to the title of *Zaphenath-Paneah*, meaning "Saviour", which he received from Pharaoh.

Joseph's story tells us in clear words that adversities can be used to build our road to success. Joseph could have stayed as a slave in Potiphar's house for the rest of his life, but he decided to make a difference. While in prison, he could have sat down, crying and lamenting the injustice he was a victim of. He decided, however, to draw a new plan. He was determined to rebuild his own story.

Joseph used his problems and different situations that came to him as steps to build up his career and life. In order to win, we must do the same, no matter the circumstances around us.

After studying in details the story of this well-known biblical character, I discovered that the roller coaster of my life is rather tiny comparing to the one Joseph had to ride! I also learned that his story is full of clear and efficient teachings on how to overcome life's down turns and how to better administer the upturns of one's adventure.

The following chapters explore the characteristics, concepts and situations that were decisive for Joseph's growth and success, and that we (even without the gift of dream interpretation) can also use for our own professional growth, regardless of the field, and as in the development of our qualities.

 1. Start early!

*"... Joseph, being seventeen years old, was feeding the flock with his brothers." Genesis 37:2*

I was twenty three years old when I first entered in a company to be a trainee. I was about to finish five years of engineering school, but I still needed 360 hours of practical work in a company to finish my coursework.

As in my case, every year thousands of students live the same experience. After collecting years of theoretical knowledge, these students want to put into practice what they learned, but in the first days at work or traineeships they don't feel comfortable at all.

In the workplace, no matter the area, problems do not show up clearly defined, with well-defined variables as students are used during exams.

The first reaction of a novice who faces a challenge at work is to recall an equation, a theory or a concept that was taught in school in order to solve that question. In many cases, one may feel that he knows absolutely nothing about that specific subject. Some young workers come to the conclusion that it was useless to spend so many years in school.

The theory is stored in the brain, but converting it into a productive action requires an extra skill, which can be developed at best by "doing the work."

The ancient adage is indeed true "practice makes perfect."

There is nothing better to learn a profession than applying what one has learned in the classroom.

Anyone could say this is obvious and I shouldn't waste time talking about that, but reality is different.

As an example, just few universities offer students the opportunity to be in contact with real work environment as trainees before the end of the studies, much less in the beginning.

Only a small number of students search independently for opportunities to work as trainees during the first years of university.

The sooner one starts gaining experience in the workplace, the less difficulties it will be to learn how to apply theoretical concepts.

The first text that associates Joseph to his work mentions his age. The text clearly says he was seventeen years old and had already worked "feeding the flock." Some translations emphasize the idea of his age by also adding "being a young man."

Nobody knows exactly how old was Joseph when he started to work, but we read that at the age of seventeen he was already working.

In some areas of work, the younger one starts working, the better the results. We all know, for example, this is indeed true for areas such as music and languages.

In a scientific study conducted at the University of Cornell, Karl H. Kim and coworkers[1,2], used functional

Magnetic Resonance Imaging (fMRI) to determine how different languages are represented in the human brain.

They discovered that the first and the second languages are separated in a region of the brain (frontal part) known as Broca's area, which is believed to control the motor parts of the mouth, tongue and palate; obviously related to speech. In contrast, both language show very little separation in Wernicke's area (located in the rear of the brain), thought to be responsible for the comprehension of language.

Once they analyzed the brain of people who were bilingual from childhood, they noticed that both languages did not show any spatial separation in Broca's neither in Wernicke's area, indicating that at least what is related to brain activation, the same brain regions control the ability to process both languages.

This study suggests that the difficulty that adults face in learning a new language is not understanding the new words, but in the motor skills needed to form the words with the mouth and tongue. Thus, the best thing one can do to learn a language is to speak it! Although this is obvious; most language courses focus on "listening and reading."[3]

The ideal scenario for a future professional is to put him in the work environment as soon as possible, while respecting obviously the limits of each student; avoiding potential overloading.

Some universities offer programs through which students are placed in a job during the first years of study, allowing them to acquire valuable work experience early.

An example of such a program is the "Cooperative education" program, also known as "co-op", which is offered by some universities. It is a structured method of combining classroom-based education with practical work experience. The idea of incorporating practical experience to what is learned in university started with Herman Schneider (1872 – 1939), when he noticed that the traditional teaching was not enough for students of technical areas.[4]

The first university to establish such a program was the University of Cincinnati[5] in 1906.

The "co-op" provides academic credit for structured job experience, helping the young students to make the transition from theory to practical work through an active engagement. Besides that, it provides great opportunities to increase one's network.[6]

The University of Waterloo in Canada, as an example, has the largest "co-op" program in the world. In total they have eleven thousand students and three thousand employers. They also have a completely automated website for the program.

The engineering degree, which takes five years to complete, includes a "co-op" program with twenty four months of supervised work in different areas of work.[7]

To obtain more information about the "co-op" program, I contacted a chemical engineer, Dimpy Gupta, a Canadian and former student of the University of Waterloo, who now works for a well-known medical company Johnson & Johnson.

I contacted her initially by email, but we finally met in a restaurant in Zürich, where she gave me an exciting explanation of how precious the traineeship experiences are for the professional development of any young person. See the following interview.

**To what extent did the co-op program influence your decision to study at the University of Waterloo?**

**Dimpy:** Co-op was my main reason to go to Waterloo and I only applied to schools with co-op programs. I chose Waterloo over other schools because it allowed to work at more companies than other schools.

**How does the program work?**

**Dimpy:** My class alternated between school and work every four months. During the four months we were at school, we would do our full course load, plus apply to jobs, and go through formal interviews and be offered jobs like real full time jobs.

**From which semester did you start to be an intern in companies?**

**Dimpy:** I started applying to jobs three weeks after I started university and started my first job after four months of university. The other half of the school started working eight months after they started university so as to stagger the classes and share jobs.

**In how many companies did you work during your five years of studies and how long did each experience last?**

**Dimpy:** We had six co-op jobs, each of them were four months long. I decided to work at Nortel for two terms (go back to the same employer), so I worked at five companies. Because of my exchange program in Switzerland, my timings were thrown off and I worked at Surromed two months, and Novartis six months. The rest were four months each.

**No doubt that such experiences helped you a lot while you were looking for a job after you concluded your engineering degree. But did you notice any difference between you (or any other colleague who also joined the co-op program) and fresh engineers who came from traditional engineering courses?**

**Dimpy:** Yes, lots of differences - we have a more practical, business-like approach, rather than academic-style thinking. Depending on the experiences, people can be more open-minded as they have seen more diversity in how companies function, and more open to traveling and relocating for work. Also, we are better prepared when applying for jobs and going through interviews. My friends who did co-op and had good co-op jobs got better and higher paying jobs than my other friends who did not do co-op (but I suppose this is also related to the fields they chose, and not representative 100% of the time). The point is the experience that the individual is driven to seek and create, rather than the co-op program itself... co-op was an opportunity to make things easier and create options, but it isn't a magic ticket.

**You mentioned two companies from different areas Nortel (Telecommunications) and Novartis (Pharma). What did you learn at Nortel that helped you at Novartis and still today in the biomedical field?**

**Dimpy:** Besides statistics, soft skills and team work, I also learned how to work in a clean room (which can be even more controlled than in the medical field). Before Nortel I worked for a mining company where I typically worked with very large equipment. Nortel was a good transition to start working with smaller/bench scale equipment and test equipment.

**In a mining company too? How was it?**

**Dimpy:** Yes, in mining of coal, where I worked in the cyanidation unit, using a more environmentally friendly process, as you know mining is very dirty work. I was even collecting samples during the night shifts.

**Why did you go back to Nortel?**

**Dimpy:** Going back gave me the opportunity to solidify and build upon my previous learnings. Under the supervision of an engineer I optimized machines and wrote reports. In the interview for my current job, I mentioned a data analysis program that I created during my co-op and my interviewer (my current boss) got very excited about using this tool for the company. That shows how important it is to solidify what you have learned in the past. Actually now I want to have my own co-op students.

**If you had the opportunity to go back in time, what would you have done differently?**

**Dimpy:** I would have kept better contact with my former supervisors.

Starting early with professional activities still has another advantage, which is the possibility of enrolling in a great number of different projects and from different fields.

Training in companies of different areas broadened Dimpy's knowledge horizon. Such broadening has allowed her to make connections between apparently unrelated areas, giving her the possibility to develop new skills.

Dimpy Gupta story is an excellent example for any university student. However you do not have to wait to start university to look for professional experience. It is possible to start even earlier, as a matter of fact you can even start your own business, before starting university.

In the summer 2009, I visited the city of Panevėžys (with a population of 110 thousand inhabitants) in Lithuania, where I met the young Rokas Lukosevicius, who at the age of 15 founded Rocky Skateshop company, one of the largest skateboard shops in the whole Baltic area. Today at the age of 17, he is one of the leaders for the Baltic market in commercializing products for this sport.

I also interviewed him to better understand how a teenager could develop so quickly the skills required to lead a company.

**What was your first job?**

Rokas: I started as a paperboy, delivering newspapers, while I was living in England. I was 14 back then.

**How did you come up with the idea of a skate shop?**

Rokas: I started with the idea, when I was 13. I spotted a free skateboard market in Lithuania. Before that I was looking at bigger business areas, like the wood or food industries. But at that time I was thinking that such markets were already taken.

**Do you have an idea of how many skateboarders exist in the Baltic? How big is the market?**

Rokas: I believe there are between 3000 and 5000 skateboarders in the Baltic and 1000 in Lithuania alone. Lithuania's market is very small and I have to work almost with each client individually in order to get an idea of what goods they want and so on. A lot of hard work is needed for a small market.

**What is your market share and how long did it take to become profitable?**

**Rokas:** I think I have taken 60-80% of the Lithuanian market. Really my business became profitable as soon as I sold my first decks.

**How did you get money to start your shop?**

**Rokas:** Working as a paperboy in the UK, I started my business with 200 euros.

**Have you learned anything from your first job, delivering newspapers, that helps you today?**

**Rokas:** The paperboy job taught me how bad life can get if you don't go to school.

**Running a business requires a lot of different skills, from organization, sales, dealing with distributors and employees, taxes, etc. What is (or was) the most complicated thing for you?**

**Rokas:** The most complicated work is with the Lithuania's customs. Since I import goods from the US, every time I need to "push" really hard to get everything running smooth.

**How did the clients react when they saw such a young entrepreneur?**

**Rokas:** My clients' reaction was very normal. Customers care more about the items they are buying than the seller.

**How do you manage your time between school and business?**

**Rokas:** It is easy! I have plenty of time after school.

**What are your plans for the future?**

**Rokas:** I am thinking about starting a new business in Greenland. Climate change is opening new lands!!!

**If you could go back in time, what would you have done differently?**

**Rokas:** If I had to start all over again, I would work much harder. Success comes ONLY with hard work.

Delivering newspapers not only showed Rokas how important it is to go to school, it was everything he needed to obtain enough funding to start his own business without needing loan.

The best time for a future entrepreneur to get prepared for his own business is while working for someone else. The future entrepreneur will have the opportunity to accumulate knowledge and funding to avoid loans.

The stories of Dimpy and Rokas, regardless of the differences, have something in common that was vital for their success: Starting early!

In the specific case of the young Joseph, we see his administrative skills were developed when he was feeding his father's flock. Betrayed by his brothers and sold by the Ishmaelites, he ends up as a slave in the house of an important Egyptian official. There he had the opportunity to show his abilities, where he became the butler or "manager" of the house. Joseph literally "took office" administering all Potiphar's goods, as the text says:

*"Now Joseph had been taken down to Egypt. And Potiphar, an officer of Pharaoh, captain of the guard, an Egyptian, bought him from the Ishmaelites who had taken him down there. The LORD was with Joseph, and he was a successful man; and he was in the house of his master the Egyptian. And his master saw that the Lord was with him and that the Lord made all he did to prosper in his hand. So Joseph found favor in his sight, and served him. Then he made him overseer of his house, and all that he had he put under his authority. So it was, from the time that he had made him overseer of his house and all that he had, that the LORD blessed the Egyptian's house for Joseph's sake; and the blessing of the LORD was on all that he had in the house and in the field. 6 Thus he left all that he had in Joseph's hand, and he did not know what he had except for the bread which he ate..."*
*Genesis 39: 1-6*

Although Joseph was doing an excellent work in the house, he lost his position, when he was falsely accused of sexual assault by his master's wife.

For the second time, Joseph had lost everything he had built.

Losing a job can be devastating for most of us. Been fired and arrested is an awful experience for everyone. But as a person who was born to be leader, Joseph found strength to stand up, to start again and to rebuild his own story.

In the prison, he conquered the trust of the prison's keeper, who appointed him to be the prison's "manager."

Joseph accepted the challenge to administer the prison, doing the best he could. Any person who wants to improve his talents or to become a leader or even who wants to be an example in what he is doing, must be willing to manager all opportunities or challenges that come up, no matter if it is a country, a company or a prison. Every and each project must be faced as an opportunity to gain experience, to grow, to learn and to contribute for the success of that particular endeavor.

Joseph was not happy to do only what was needed, he was willing to go beyond and to make the work better. Remember that he did not go to the prison to become a manager, but he entered as a common prisoner. However he knew that he was not born to be a prisoner, thus he looked for opportunities to grow. He did not wait to be a minister to show his talents. He did not wait for the "opportunity of a lifetime", he took advantage of the "small" opportunities to build up his career to the top.

In the development of leadership and project management skills, nothing is more precious than practical experiences, for example leading small groups at school, work, church or even in children's sport team in your community.

The disposition to manage "little projects" with seriousness can be very helpful when the opportunity comes to make decisions on big projects.

Although "small projects" may be in different areas, certain skills are common for all areas. Team working, conflict resolution and task assignment are examples of common skills in all areas of administration. Therefore do not disregard any opportunity!

Who would have imagined that a shepherd was prepared to become the leader of another country?

The first lesson a young person must learn with Joseph's story is that, in order to stand out as a professional it is important to start early to obtain practical experience.

If you still have no professional experience or just started as university or technical student, consider looking for a job or internship opportunity as soon as possible, even if you do not receive monetary compensation. You must understand this is the time to invest in your future career. The experience you will obtain in "small" projects can be foundational steps for your professional growth.

Besides that you will rule out the number one barrier for any novice in the search for a job: Lack of professional experience!

In the appendix of this book, there is a list of professions and university courses with examples of places where one can look for an internship position to complement one's education. I have also presented a series of suggestions of "little" projects that can be executed to impel the career of a novice.

It is then up to you to strive to find such opportunities, because you should be the most interested person in your own success.

Start as soon as possible!


*"Those who recognize science in the humblest work will see in it nobility and beauty, and will take pleasure in performing it with faithfulness and efficiency."*

*Ellen G. White*
*(Counsels to Parents, Teachers, and Students)*

 ## 2. Body language

*"And Joseph came in to them in the morning and looked at them, and saw that they were sad. So he asked Pharaoh's officers who were with him in the custody of his lord's house, saying, "Why do you look so sad today?" Genesis 40: 6 - 7*

During the investigations of a rape case in a Indian Reservation in the US, one of the suspects was interrogated by the FBI agent, Joe Navarro. The suspect's words were convincing and everything indicated he was innocent, however the agent noticed that while the suspect explained that he had not seen the victim that day and when he was in the field had "turned left", his hand, however, gestured to the right, which was exactly the way to the crime scene. That "small" discrepancy between the suspect's words and his body language made the agent realize that something was wrong, and that the man was lying. After been confronted again, he admitted the crime!

This is one of the first cases described by Joe Navarro in his book "What every BODY is saying"[1], which quickly became a classic on the subject of body language.

Similarly in the prison, Joseph noticed, when entering the cell of Pharaoh's officials, that something was wrong, just by looking at their faces. So he persisted with those men, that they could declare to him, what was disturbing them.

Roger Ailes, co-author of the book, "You are the Message: Secrets of Master Communicators", who was also media consultant for several US presidents, claims that "facial expression is often the most difficult area of nonverbal communication to master because we are taught early that our faces can give us away. Many people particularly business executives, freeze their faces regardless of emotional state they are in."

It is very common to notice a friend, companion, coworker or a relative showing in his face an expression of worry, anger or fear, but once asked what is going on, we hear something like: "Everything is fine!"

Thanks to his ability to understand body language, Joseph, opened up the doors for a change in his life. Joseph's gift of dream interpretation would have never been famous, if he had not firstly used the skills to interpret body expressions.

The proper reading of body language is probably one of the most important skills for professional growth, regardless of the field. Those who understand body language; understand what is happening around, without words.

You must learn body language communication in order to know when is the right time to speak, to be quite, to know when to act or to leave. In short to make the right decision to obtain the best result.

Given that there is vast literature[1-12] available around the topic of body language, it is not the aim of this book to enter into the details of this subject. However it is important to emphasize that the ability to understand body language is not only an excellent too for professional growth, but essential for a leader.

"What happened?" "What is really going on?" "Why are you upset?" Such questions can open the way to great discoveries.

In a famous study conducted by Albert Mehrabian[13], it was found that only 7% of communication comes from spoken words, while 38% from the tone of the voice and 55% from the body language. One must know, however that Mehrabian was referring to cases where feelings and attitudes were expressed.[14]

It is also important to consider the individuals who suffer from some sort of behavior disability (autistics, as an example, have a development disability that affect communication and emotional reciprocity) use and interpret body language in a different manner. Therefore, to interpret their gestures and facial expressions in the normal context of body language may lead to misunderstanding. The same can happen with people from different cultural background, where their body language is influenced by local social and cultural factors, who may not only use, in some cases a different body language from ours, but for the same reason could also wrongly interpret ours.[15] One can say, therefore, that it is important to understand the cultural, social and even psychological factors for a proper communication and understanding.

Even if limited in some way, a leader must learn how to correctly "read" and "speak" body language. Therefore do not ignore the nonverbal communication!

Anyone who disregards a nonverbal message may, in fact, be ignoring a very important piece of information of what is truly happening around.

The ability to understand body language becomes crucial in the corporate world, where leaders wrongly believe that they can obtain all information they need just because they have the authority.

Unfortunately just a few employees are willing to give all available information or news to a leader, specially if the news are not good news.

In 1991 John Byrne coined the expression "CEO disease"[16], defined as "an information vacuum around a leader, created when people withhold important (and usually unpleasant) information." In other words, usually a leader does not receive all important information, specially the bad news!

Why do workers do that? An obvious reason is the fact that nobody likes to be a bearer of bad news.

In his book "The New Leaders"[17], Daniel Goleman analyses this fact, showing that the "CEO disease" is even more common among leaders who have a commanding style. For this reason, some subordinates decide to deliver good news only, since they are afraid to be symbolically executed. Others only give good and pleasant news to be seen as "good citizens" or because they are afraid to be considered as "heretics".

Whatsoever the reason is, the result is a leader deprived of information, knowing only partially what is happening around him. Such a problem can become epidemic, and it is fed by the natural desire to "please the boss".[17]

The higher a leader's position is, the less likely he will receive all needed information.[15] This situation becomes worst when the leader is a woman or a member of a minority group.[17, 19-21]

One of the ways to avoid the "CEO disease" is to master the art of nonverbal communication.

The ability of proper reading the body language becomes indispensable for any professional who must do public speaking. The larger the audience is, the greater the number of nonverbal messages that must be understood by the speaker.[22] Eyebrow frown, to leaf through books or journals, side conversations and texting are just some examples of how the audience start to "protest" against the speaker or against the message.

Therefore, anyone who has to do public speaking, must be prepared to attract and to keep the listeners' attention. Body language is, in this as in other cases, one of the best tools. Since our eyes tend to follow the hand movements[1] (this is how the conjurers use their hands to distract us while performing their tricks), a great way to keeping the audience's attention is to be more expressive with the hands.

If you have an opportunity, watch a video from a famous public speaker and observe how he uses his hands to explain his ideas.

While I was in Canada, I had the opportunity to meet Bill Santos, director and presenter of a famous TV program called "It is Written."

Bill has a degree in Theology and worked for 17 years as a Business Consultant, but since 2004 he leads and presents the Program.

Every week, Bill is seen by thousands of people either on TV or by Internet. His program is presented in Portuguese and English, therefore his work is well known not only in the US and Canada, but also in the Portuguese speaking countries such as Brazil, Portugal, Angola, Mozambique, Cape Verde and others.

Bill spends hours in front of a camera, without having any idea about the audience's reaction. The message he presents to the public is not only in his words, but also in his gestures and facial expressions. I decided to talk to Bill about the relevance of body language in his profession.

**What is the relevance of body language in your work?**

**Bill:** 93% of what people take from my message and what they will remember about me (and you and everyone) is based on what you look like and what you sound like, with the words you use accounts for the remaining 7%. Of that 93% - the body language is 55%. When there is a contradiction between your words and your tone and body language, people will always go to tone and body language for the real message.

**Due to your professional background you have experience to adjust your body language to your spoken words. But where is more complicated to "speak" the right body language: in front of cameras or crowds and why?**

**Bill:** Since the bulk of the speaking that I did and do is in front of alive audience that environment became more "natural" for me thus easier for me to look and feel less rigid. The television studio is rather "un-natural" for me so I must force myself to visualize an audience and I must be very comfortable with the material or else my body language will come off a little forced.

**What are the most common "suggestions" that an audience sends via body language to a speaker when they are losing interest in the speech?**

**Bill:** Throwing rotten vegetables is probably the most clear indication!!! Seriously though, I tend to monitor how much the audience is "fidgeting" that tends to be a sign to me that my message and their needs are not in alignment. Communication theory tells us that people will only listen to a message that touches upon their needs, values or goals. So to me, if an audience is not "listening" it says to me that my audience analysis was somehow flawed and my message is not connecting with the audience. It becomes more about me than about the audience.

**It is common to see public speakers feeling uncomfortable with their hands. The so famous "I-don't-know-where-to-put-my-hands." Could you give some practical advices for young professionals who need to be in an interview or to deliver a speech but are not sure how to control their body language?**

Bill: If you are in a one-to-one setting, like a job interview and you are nervous and do not want your body language to show that, then you can use a technique called "mirroring." Simply, mirroring is when you take your body language cues from the other person. In other words, you mimic their body language (with discretion) on a 30 second delay. You basically do what they are doing, but you do it 30 seconds after they have done. If they lean forward, you lean forward after 30 seconds, if they placed their hands on their laps, you copy 30 seconds later, and so one. This is done when they are doing the bulk of the talking. When it is your turn to talk, to stop mimicking and you take the lead and you watch to see if they are mimicking you back, if they are you can know you have a "connection" with them. In public we tend to suggest that you practice your body language in front of a mirror, looking for any gestures that might present a message that is contradictory to what you are saying. Remember that people will turn to the body language for the real content of the message. This says to me that the most important things when speaking in public with the intent to influence your audience are, preparation, integrity and confidence (not necessarily in that order).

**We know that not only the gestures and facial expressions transmit the message, but the hair style, what you wear, etc. What are in your opinion the three or five items you consider the most relevant in the body language of someone who wants to be seen as trustworthy?**

**Bill:** In terms of dress, you are better to be "over dressed" than "under dressed" - you are better off being more formal and then realizing that you could have dressed more casual than vice versa. Eye contact is key – when speaking to a large audience make sure you "scan" the entire audience. If speaking to a small group - you should make eye contact with everyone but your eyes should always return to the decision maker.

The proper understanding of body language is not only useful in a professional arena, but in some cases can be the only way to avoid a tragedy. Through this language, a woman could more likely notice if the person who is approaching her is a potential rapist or thief, before he is too near to attack. Observing the children's behavior, parents could discover if the kids are involved with drugs or other illegal activities, before it is too late to solve the problem. Also through the body language, spouses could notice when something wrong is happening in the relationship, having then the opportunity to work it out before it goes too far.

Some people or certain groups of people have better skills to understand the body language than others. It was observed that in some cases this phenomenon is influenced by the environment where the people live or their cultural background. People who belong to discriminated groups, as an example, have a more accurate ability to notice if someone is acting with prejudice just through the body language.

In 1978, Steven A. Rollman published an excellent article, showing that Afro-Americans are more capable to perceive non verbal cues with discriminatory content than their white compatriots.[23] The most interesting part of this study was to show that the Afro-Americans interpret the body language of the white people better than the white people among themselves. The potential reasons for such result can be, among others:

1) Culture. It is believed that more gestural cultures interpret more accurately the body movements.[24]

2) Experience!

The Afro-Americans gesticulate more and they were for many centuries victims of discrimination, what made them more perceptive to catch and decipher discriminatory body messages sent by others.

This principle can probably be also applied to people who live in dangerous areas or under constant stress. Through the emission of nonverbal messages, such people develop the ability to perceive an approaching adverse situation.

However, anyone who desires to understand body language must be ready to observe what is happening around. It is also important to constantly practice a judicious observation to learn how to distinguish the nonverbal information. To better develop such skills, it is important to do a careful study of the theory around nonverbal communication and to daily observe how the mechanisms of such a "language" work.

The understanding and mastering of this language will be a valuable tool, which will help you build up a brilliant future or to escape from dangerous situations. The references 1 to 22 (see References) list a series of books and websites that deal with this subject and can be helpful with learning about body language. I want, however, to make known that I do not endorse neither agree with all theories, techniques or suggestions presented in the references. Therefore, it is important that you learn how to "filter" the information presented in such books and websites, to compare with other sources, as well as to observe or test by yourself if such techniques are indeed trustworthy. Consider, however the fact, that the movement of the hands, a fake smile, positioning of the feet or eye blinking are not enough to make conclusions. They only help to show that there is a possibility. Therefore be cautious when "reading" the body language to make conclusions, likewise be cautious once reading the literature on this subject. Remember that the word 'probably' does not mean 100%.

A discerning observation of the body language is an excellent tool for professional life, but as in any other area of life, if this tool is wrongly used it can become detrimental, potentially creating a disturbed person, or even a paranoid, who hastily jump into wrong conclusions and wrongly judge people's intentions and everything around. Therefore, be cautious, but do not ignore this important tool.

*"The evidence shows that when our bodies are saying something different from our mouths it is our bodies which are telling the truth"*
*Venon Coleman, (People Watching)*

# 3. Network

*"But remember me when it is well with you, and please show kindness to me; make mention of me to Pharaoh, and get me out of this house." Genesis 40:14*

It is very hard to achieve professional success without the help from friends, relatives, acquaintances or colleagues, or from friends of friends. In other words, without a social network, accessing professional life is very arduous.

I have recently carried out a quick survey among friends, colleagues and relatives from various professional backgrounds, such as engineers, teachers, secretaries, journalists, accountants, farmers, etc. where I sent them an email with a short questionnaire asking them how they got their first, second and current job. The questionnaire that I prepared can be seen below.

1- How did you get your first job?

     a) Through someone from your network.

     b) Sending the Curriculum Vitae (CV) directly to a job offer or agent.

2- How did you get your second job?

     a) Through someone from your network.

     b) Sending the Curriculum Vitae (CV) directly to a job offer or agent.

3- How did you get your current job?

     a) Through someone from your network.

     b) Sending the Curriculum Vitae (CV) directly to a job offer or agent.

I have sent this short questionnaire by email to all my contacts as well as to the virtual groups that I belong to. With this quick survey I wanted to verify if in the process of seeking and finding the first, second and current job, a tendency could be found that characterizes the process of changing jobs while growing in the profession.

The result could not be more obvious. The number of people who obtained their first job just by submitting their CV as an answer to a job posting or through an agent was 41%, while the network accounted for 59%. In other words, most people get first job through their personal network, either through a close friend, relative, colleague or an acquaintance.

The question about the second job showed very similar results. However, the current job (it could be third, forth, etc.) showed an increase in the number of those who marked the network option. In fact, 62% declared that they had obtained their current job through their network. This result indicates that while we grow in our professional life we expand our network, increasing the chances that our next professional move will be done with the help from someone who belongs on our contact list.

The result of my survey did not differ much from the results that Mark Granovetter[1] obtained in his famous work, "Getting a job", where he found that 56% of the people he interviewed got their jobs through their network. The most interesting parts of his work was the observation that from those (56%) who got a job through their network, only 16.7% saw their contact on a regular basis. He then coined the expression the "strength of weak ties."

Malcom Gladwell in his bestseller, "The tipping point"[2] emphasizes that when it comes to finding a job, our social "weak ties" are more important than our strong ties, since our close friends and relatives basically live in the same "world" we live in, knowing what we know and working where we work, while an acquaintance lives in another "world", which we have little access.

Fairs, conferences and analogous are excellent events to expand the number of acquaintances in your network, which can have an enormous value in the future.

It is actually almost impossible to predict which new contact will bring the greatest benefit; whether it be someone whom you just met in a conference or a stranger who sat by your side at the church or at the theater. Therefore do not overlook any opportunity to expand your network. But we shouldn't forget that some individuals can have superb performance as elements of a network. They are the ones who can put us in contact with "key players." in Joseph's case, it was Pharaoh's chief butler!

When I planned my little email survey I didn't intend to statistically verify the power of networks, neither to revise Granovetter's results. The authentic reason behind my research was to find out how many of my contacts would naturally be prone to answer my questions. From over a thousand people in my email list, to whom I sent the email, only 5.7% answered my request. Among those who didn't answer the survey, there were close friends, relatives and former co-workers. It doesn't mean they neglected my request, because they didn't care about me, but just that not all of them had the same availability or disposition to help. Or maybe they did not consider my request with the same relevance as the 5.7% did. Or maybe they didn't have time for that. Moreover, among the ones who didn't answer, there was no difference in gender, neither between old and more recent friends.

There is a lesson to be learned: the simple fact that you have a big network, doesn't mean you can always count on these people, since not everyone in your network has all the qualities or characteristics that make the profile of a collaborator.

The trust in one's network is, in fact, one of the biggest mistakes committed by those who want to use their networks as a trampoline to grow professionally. This is typical in the political world. Teachers, professors, businessmen and others, who believe they "know" everyone in the city, are easily convinced that they will win an election when they look at the size of their network.

It is not the size of the network that matters, but the quality!

I have a friend, Almir da Costa, who is a teacher, writer, speaker and director of the biggest public library in his city. He also has a long list of friends, colleagues, collaborators from schools, social projects and churches, and with a reputation above suspicion; he decided to run in the municipal election for the board of Aldermen.

After months of a stressful campaign, the result could not be more disappointing; only 1044 votes in his first election, and only 744 when he tried for the second time.

In Mossoró (in the state of Rio Grande do Norte, Brazil), where he lives, a city of approximately 250 thousand people, he would need only 1950 votes to be elected. How could it be possible that he, with so many friends, colleagues and potential collaborators did not win, while others, who are not as well known by the public and with smaller networks claimed victory?

I talked to Almir da Costa about his experience and I would like to publisher this interview below.

**To what extent did the large number of people you know make you believe that you had a "guaranty" to be victorious in the elections? Moreover, you listened to many people saying they would vote for you. Why, in your option, they promised something, but did something else?**

**Almir:** In politics, not always the large number of friends can make a difference. For many people, a friend is a friend, while a candidate is a candidate. In the other hand, the political clientelism speaks very loudly; money and the buying of votes dictate the rules of an election, of the future decisions and how everything will finish. For example, people who deserved a position at the board of Aldermen in our city, or anywhere else in the country lost the election from one day to the next. When they thought it was all decided, the money came and changed everything.

We live in a very corrupted and corrupting world, but we who try to do everything right, are walking against the wave.

Therefore, to be well-known, doing good to all, making as many friends as possible, among other virtues, do not guaranty victory in an election. Without the money's command, which is the driving-force, just a very few people could claim victory. Thus, the well-intended candidates, pay a very high price for their defeat in the elections! In this framework, I repeat, with few exceptions, money determines the winner, no matter what you represent to the society. It reminds me of an old saying: "In politics and business, there is no honesty."

**Does money alone defines the results of an election? How do you explain cases of candidates without the power of money, who won, even in poor areas, where the buying of votes is commonplace? What would be the other factors that influence the results of an election?**

**Almir:** Yes, money decides any campaign. See this example: when I negotiate with you for your vote, you give the exact location where you are registered to vote. So, I know if you voted or not for me. If in that location there were not votes for me, it means you didn't vote for me as we agreed, then my commitment with you is canceled. This way, the voter is trapped. You may ask: why? If I am a candidate and I promise you a bicycle after the elections, you will do everything you can do that I win, because you need and you want this bicycle. This is just a simple example, there are much bigger commitments; this is what we call political clientelism.

There are some rare exceptions. At the end, in business and politics there is no honesty, no respect... it may happen to win an election without money, but very rarely. The people together has enough force to decide anything: in politics, in other social matters, etc. But in some cases, the money speaks louder than words, dictates the rules, determines the fate.

**Years later, your wife, a well-know physician in the city, accepted the call of friends and acquaintances to run for the elections. The story repeated itself! What happened this time?**

**Almir:** It is true. After trying twice, without victory, I handed over the task to my wife, who after been encouraged by me and others, accepted the challenge. We did a great work. We jumped into the campaign, visited street after street, house after house. We showed our project for the local community in the case she would be elected. We presented the best proposals, but for our surprise, she didn't get even the minimum of the minimum. We obtained less than we could imagine.

We spent days and days thinking where it went wrong. What didn't we do? But the problem was not in our work, everything was made with order and correctness, with honesty and clear objectives. We concluded that, unfortunately her voters sold themselves to anyone who offered immediate advantages: money, bricks, tiles, bicycles and other tools of corrupted politics. We decided not to work like that. We have money, but we would never use it to corrupt people. We were always very clear, and maybe this was one of the reasons for my wife's defeat in the election. Given that we still live in culture with a crazy political clientelism, we decided to call it quits. We gave up with politics.

**What was the biggest mistake during the campaigns?**

**Almir:** As I said before, in a campaign there are many pros and cons. In the middle of all, we end up making different mistakes.

As a matter of fact, putting your trust in a specific group of people, during a campaign, turns out to be a fatal mistake for any candidate. You should never think that your campaign is fine, that you have everything under control. This happened to me and with others who thought like me. In a campaign for public offices such as for the board of Aldermen, major, deputy, etc. you must have in mind that if you think you have ten thousand votes, you then must work to get double or triple of that, or even four or five times as many votes. Only then will you have a chance. If the political clientelism doesn't enter in your "garden" and buy your votes. If this does happen, everything can go down, since against the power of money there is no defense. As I said before with rare exceptions.

Another mistake during a campaign is to be transparent, to tell the truth. Many politicians win the elections through lies and promises that will never be fulfilled after elections. As a simple example, there was a candidate, who during the campaign, printed thousands of health insurance cards, saying that, if elected, he would provide medical assistance during his four years of mandate. As a result he won. He then started to fulfill his promise, but slowly he decreased the medical assistance for a very small number of people. In the following election he ran again, but didn't win, because he lost the people's trust.

Many politicians also win, while promising jobs and other benefits, this is well-known by all. This happens very often. There are other ways to win by deceiving the voters. But I never did such misconducts.

These were the mistakes, if we can call them mistakes, that I committed during my campaigns. Or that I didn't do during my campaigns.

**I think you touched on a crucial point when you mentioned that "Putting your trust in a specific group of people, during a campaign, turns out to be a fatal mistake for any candidate." Since you have summarized what I consider one of the biggest mistakes of new politicians or candidates, "putting the trust in their network", given that the others do not see our dreams and projects as we see them. Based on what you learned, what would be the**

best for a candidate, to spend the energy solidifying the contacts that he has or looking for new associates?

**Almir:** New associates and supporters of your project can make a difference in your campaign. But, they will not work "for free" for your. They want something from you after election; your promise, your commitment. This also means political clientelism. If many people help you and work for you, you may achieve your goals. It can also happen that you may win just by a collective awareness work, etc. This is not easy, but can happen. But don't forget: This is very rare!

**Before joining the first campaign, did you have any practical experience helping other politicians?**

**Almir:** No, I entered directly, after being invited by the major of city back then, who today is a federal senator. But in politics, don't expect for help. It is a situation where "everybody for himself, and God for all."

Politicians also, but rarely, may promise to help in your campaign, before the elections of course. After the election, you are alone again. They may invest in some politicians and use others to be elected.

Do not believe in politicians! This is the advice of a good friend. An old man told me once: "a poor man who believes in politicians, is poor and crazy!"

Almir's answers made me curious to discover if politicians from other countries, with a lower level of corruption than Brazil, face the same problem of political clientelism that Almir faced.

I decided then to contact and interview a German politician, who had been defeated in the last elections. Since 2009 was a year of elections, it wasn't a hard task to find someone.

In the streets of Mainz I saw a billboard from a politician that got my attention. Erwin Schott, candidate from the state of Rhine-Palatinate, affiliated to a party called "Violets", which has an interesting slogan: "For a spiritual politics." Erwin is involved with politics since 2006, and in his own words, his party "considers spirituality an element of collaboration in politics." Besides the TV program and a website on the Internet, the party also contacted people on the streets and visited fairs and exhibitions, they also placed information booths in the big centers. Obviously they also placed the famous billboards in strategic places.

I asked him about money and elections in Germany, besides other aspects of German politics, as you can read in the following lines.

**There are countries that, due to corruption, money "alone" can define the results of an election. How is the relationship between money and politics in Germany?**

**Erwin:** The big parties receive money directly from the state. The bigger the party is, the larger the amount of money. The CDU (Christian-Democratic Union) and particularly the FDP (Free Democratic Party), as a "business party", receive large donations from the business world. This way, they can do intensive advertisement.

**Is there in Germany any scheme for buying votes?**

**Erwin:** What is that?

(Well, it seems that this is not the problem that the German politicians face!)

**Is it enough to just be known and to have many friends in order to get elected?**

**Erwin:** No. The program of the party is fundamental. Friends and acquaintances help only in the moment of collecting supporting signatures.

**How important it is to have a "good contact"?**

**Erwin:** This is what characterizes the parties that represent the German Government. We want to change this! That is what we are here for.

**What are the most important characteristics that candidates must have? Charisma? Intelligence? Rhetoric?**

**What should the profile of a new candidate be in order to be successful?**

**Erwin:** I believe authenticity and credibility. Rhetoric surely helps, as well as all the other points you mentioned. However the candidate must personalize authenticity. It is also very important to write and speak German without any mistakes. But the essential is to be fully committed.

**Do you have any advice for the next generation of candidates? What the newcomers should learn to be victorious?**

**Erwin:** To give more personal recommendations, I would need more experience in politics. Therefore I can't give any specific answers for this question. But, one thing I am sure about: it is important to be identified with the program and party's ideology, and to "live them", as I said before, to be fully committed!

From the cases of Almir da Costa and Erwin Schott, I have definitely learned that honesty and large networks do not grand any victory in politics. As the size of the network, as well as the other characteristics such as authenticity and honesty are not enough to be victorious, money alone is not the solution. Victory is obtained by the combination of a series of factors such as:

- An excellent marketing campaign (which can be obtained with money);
- Charisma;
- Money (in some cases, a lot of money!);
- Luck ;
- Supporters from the media;
- The current 'hot topic'.

I didn't put the factor "number of friends", because you shouldn't deceive yourself, thinking that the fact that you have many friends and acquaintances is all you need to win an election or to be free from unemployment. As shown before, there are many other factors that can determine the fate of an election, or the foundation of a company or the success of any other project.

I will however add another element, which is more important than the number of contacts:

### The contact!

Contacts are not as important as "the contact."

As Erwin Schott declared, the leading parties in Germany are characterized for having "good contacts." Unfortunately it will be very hard to change this reality. Therefore, do not start your project trusting in the number of friends, or in the members of your club or church. You will probably need them, but do not make yourself dependent on them! Consider the fact that you will have to conquer them to support your project, but do not deceive yourself with promises; you must find resources and methods to conquer supporters in order to become victorious.

The large number of friends that you have, will be of no use, if they are not committed with your project. And above all, you should remember that much more important than many contacts, you must look for "the contact!" To better understand this point, let's go back to my survey.

Probably the number of people, who answered my questionnaire, would have been larger if I had sent individual emails for each person and not for groups of people, given that when a message is sent to a group, the individuals are prone to regard the message as less important, and a certain "laziness" takes control, since the person who receives the email, thinks the others will answer, therefore he thinks there is no problem if he doesn't reply.

There are, however, individuals who are naturally prone to answer, and these are exactly the ones, who could make a difference, in political campaign, or while you are looking for a job or starting your own business.

In the end, what matters is not size of the network, but the quality of it. And, as I said some individuals can make a difference in a network!

Malcolm Gladwell[2] identifies three classes of people who are responsible for sparking "social epidemics", being then, excellent members for a network. People who will influence others who have immense networks, and who could easily promote your restaurant, to energize your political endeavor, your cultural event, or to put you in contact with the right person from the company you want to work for. The three classes of people are:

- Connectors
- *Mavens*
- Salesmen

According to Malcolm Gladwell, connectors are those people who have a great ability to make friends and acquaintances. They have friends in the political world, industry and in the media. They have contacts with people from the most different areas. They know the doorkeeper and the cleaner of their children's school as well as the director of a multi million company. When you mention about a new restaurant, they already know the owner.

The second group of people is formed by *Mavens*. This term, comes from the Yiddish, a language spoken mainly by the Jews in Central and East Europe, which means "he who accumulates knowledge." *Mavens* are individuals who know which supermarket has the best sales, which hotels offer best services, the prices, down to the cents!

*Mavens* are not only accumulators of information, they are also active transmitters of information! They let the friends know where the best places to go shopping are, where specific products are cheaper, etc. also letting the friends know where the prices are high.

They know the details of the credit card contracts and warn their friends about the potential pitfalls of some credit cards and banks. They like to read the promotional fryers that are places in the mailboxes.

With the natural disposition or inclination to help, *Mavens*, end up creating a mouth-to-mouth marketing campaign. And, since they are active and always seen as honest people, they develop the ability to attract attention, and without pressure, convince people of their ideas and opinions, filled with statistics and facts.

You can do a quick search by yourself. Look for information in the Internet, about any hotel, and you will find web pages where people rate the hotel and exchange stories. Read the comments and you will quickly recognize who the *Mavens* of that page are, behind the detailed comments and useful advices for anyone who is seeking information about that specific hotel.

Thus, for Gladwell, *Mavens* are data banks, message bearers, while the connectors the social glue, the ones who spread the message.

The third group of selected people are the "Salesmen", these are the ones who can persuade us, when we are not yet convinced of something. People with some charming and contagious enthusiasm, who make the others want to agree with what they say!

Expanding a network is a must for any potential leader. To collect business cards becomes the new hobby of anyone who wants to grow professionally. But to find the right people for one's network is an art to be developed.

In most of the cases, people from your network are not the solution for your problem, however many of them, may know someone how has the answer for what you are looking for. Thus, it is important to obtain as much as possible from each contact. Hill and Power[3], suggest for example, that in the search for an investment for a business, the leader must learn how to transform each "no" in at least one or two new contacts. "If you are not interested in a company like mine you could indicate to me one or two other people who potentially could be?" This way, you are taking advantage of the fact that investors know investors, and they can connect you to other potential investors. You are also making use of the psychology of rejection in your favor, since most people do not like to say "no", so, when you ask them for one or two names of investors who could be interested, you are turning a "no" into something that your interlocutor will have the feeling he is helping.[3]

Most venture capital investors, for example, do not invest in companies that have not been introduced by someone from their own network.

When we started our search for an investor for our first company, Smart Biotech (developer of technologies for the treatment of cerebral aneurysms), in Toronto, Canada, we looked in the Internet for the telephone numbers of companies that could potentially be interested in investing in a company like ours. However, it was not enough to call the companies and to send our business plan, we had to create stronger connections with potential investors. We started to join meetings, where new entrepreneurs got together to exchange experiences, trying to find new names, new leads and new opportunities, hoping also to meet the friend of a friend of an investor.

In such a meeting, we found the contact of an Angel Investors association from Toronto. We submitted our business plan and we were invited to present our project, but we weren't successful in securing investment. But we didn't give up, but we just kept searching.

We were invited for the second time to present our project to a group of investors, but once again we failed.

We were having the feeling that we had already "contacted everyone."

Although Internet seems to be a boundless source of information, it has an "ocean" of low quality information and sometimes is almost impossible to find something precise or trustful information. Therefore the personal contact with someone who knows "someone" is still the best way to create something fruitful.

There are many ways to increase your network. Do no limit yourself to Internet search engines or the traditional or obvious routes.

While we still believed in our project (Smart Biotech), we kept looking for opportunities to meet people who could help us.

I accepted for example, a suggestion from a friend called Darrell Stanley. He used to play golf and once took me along, to be his caddy. His idea was that, while I was working as a caddy, I could get in contact with millionaires or potential investors, since golf is highly appreciated by them. My good friend was neither CEO nor millionaire, but an excellent golfer, which created a lot of interaction with other players. I, on the other hand, had no idea about golf.

During the game, between strokes, I had opportunities to interact with the players, creating new contacts.

My experience in the golf course that day did not solve our problem, but at least I had the opportunity to meet among the players a CEO of a new company in the field of renewable energy, who was also looking for investors (apparently I was not the only one with the hope to meet a millionaire that morning!), and during our conversation I obtained the contact of other potential investors.

The most important thing, however from that day, was to learn that creating a new contact in such a situation (in a golf course, or any other activity, such as sports, religious or social) is very beneficial, because in such situations, one can create a very strong link, something like the beginning a friendship, given that the new contact was created outside the walls of an office. People can talk more freely, without using the typical "official business language" and without the masks of the business world.

That experience also thought me valuable information and gave me practical experience with golf, something that I later used as a common link with other investors who are fans of this sport.

When Joseph interpreted the dream of the chief butler, he tried at the instant to solidify that new contact: "but remember me!" That moment could be seen as a special moment, something like the beginning of a friendship between Joseph and that man, since both of them were in the same situation as prisoners.

Even with the creation of that common element (prison) between both men and the fact that Joseph had helped him while he was in prison and also interpreted his dream; we can see that the desired result from that connection took a long time to take a place. Three days after the interpretation of the chief butler's dream, he was released from prison and got back to work, as it had been predicted by Joseph. However the chief butler didn't remember Joseph, as anyone would expect as a sign of gratitude and consideration for someone who was so helpful. The biblical text says:

*"at the end of two full years... Then the chief butler spoke to Pharaoh... there was a young Hebrew man... and he interpreted our dreams for us."*
*Genesis 41: 1, 9, 12*

In other words, it required two years for that new contact to generate a positive result for Joseph.

In fact, we can't predict how long it will take for our contacts to create the desired results. It is a mistake to think that our contacts will act right at the moment we need or want. Another big mistake is to disregard a contact, just because that person cannot help us at the moment. It is important to keep an active connection. Let the person know you still exist at least with an email once a year.

Every person has a different way of interpreting a request and determining the urgency or importance of a project. Therefore it is important to be prepared for the fact, that our contacts will not always see our projects with the same seriousness and passion that we see them. Besides that, it is almost impossible to know which contact will produce the desired results.

I can imagine Joseph, loosing all his hopes of receiving any help from the chief butler, but as in this case, sometimes a good thing comes from where we have not expected and when we were not expecting it. But when the results come or the opportunity arrives, we must be prepared to act. This is what will discuss in the next chapter.


*"Eventually everything connects – people, ideas, objects. The quality of the connection is the key to the quality per se."*
Charles Eames

# 4. First impression

*"Then Pharaoh sent and called Joseph, and they brought him quickly out of the dungeon; and he shaved, changed his clothing, and came to Pharaoh." Genesis 41:14*

Our connections can and do open doors, once open, we must deliver, since as a rule, there is only one chance to make a good impression. We can't deny that "the first impression is the last impression." Obviously, there are situations, where we may get two, three or even more additional opportunities, but do not count on them! In most of the cases it is imperative to cause a favorable impression at the first meeting.

I have already interacted in many job interviews, as an interviewer as well as a job seeker, and I can affirm that in most of the cases the decision about the candidate is taken during the first minutes of the conversation. The next twenty or even sixty minutes are just formalities. Therefore, when the opportunity you are waiting for presents itself, make sure to cause the best first impression.

When Joseph was called before Pharaoh, he prepared himself for that meeting. The biblical text says that he shaved and changed his clothing. He was keenly aware of his talents to interpret dreams. He knew his skills, he was sure God was with him, but he did not leave his clothing or any other supposedly detail unattended to prepare for that meeting.

It happens quite often that the "details" divert the attention from the important things. Think of how many times you attended a presentation, a lecture, or even a concert and a small apparently "irrelevant" detail of the clothing, scenario, or any other circumstance grabbed your attention distracting your mind from the important issues. Failing to heed small details can ruin a great effort. To avoid this, Joseph, although aware of this abilities, prepared himself to the utmost, concentrating also on the finer points, minding all those small details that could dwell on the Pharaoh's attention and eventually crush that "job interview."

Certain details must be carefully taken care of before any presentation, job interview, date or political meeting.

Such as:

<u>Clothing</u>

No matter if you agree or disagree, people, in a first meeting will judge you by your clothing. In fact clothing reveals a lot about a person, therefore it is very important to observe the proper way of dressing for the occasion. If you don't know the dress code for a specific meeting, get informed beforehand.

To appear for a job interview, as a plain example, wearing too casual clothes can give the impression that you are not responsible, or even that you don't take your profession seriously, event if, in fact, you do. Remember we are talking about first impression, and if you don't succeed there, your chances to remedy that minimize afterwards.

If you cannot obtain information about the dress code for a meeting, then make the wisest decision: be conservative! It is always better to be "overdressed" than "underdressed". It is always easier to remove a tie, in case the meeting proceeds rather casual, and you are the only one wearing a tie. But if the meeting is rather formal, and you realize you are the only one in a completely different dress style, it will be tough to change that!

Certainly, being overdressed for a job interview will not kill your chances to get a job. The potential employer may even tell you that you didn't have to overdress for the meeting. But then again, the employer may choose another candidate for the position because of your inadequate clothing, either too casual, sexy or just not fitting the situation. Keep in mind, deciding for a proper clothing won't require major investments, but only prudence from your side.


*Concerning fingernails*

Dirty fingernails: By no means!
Natural or artificially extremely long nails: Again a no no!
Flashy and cheap nails: Beware!


*About hairstyle*

Comb it to adequately match your overall style, not to make it appear the most important thing in the universe. Flashy hairstyles will only prove a stumbling block during a job interview!

If you don't shave before an interview you will give the impression that you don't care too much, like it or not.

Beards and mustaches will be welcome only when neatly trimmed and in line with your overall appearance.

Hair extruding from the nostrils: Hundred times no!

<u>*Hygiene*</u>

Don't apply excessive perfume, but never go to an interview smelling badly! Ask a close friend or relative for a sincere opinion. I met a young man, who was very intelligent, with excellent marks from the university who could speak many languages, but could not get a job for the simple reason that he smelled badly! The first minutes of an interview sufficed to decide against hiring him, no matter what his qualifications. In some cases, a good shower, basic bodily hygiene and neat clothes are more important than good marks from university.

<u>*Punctuality*</u>

Thomas C. Haliburton, a Canadian writer, once said that "punctuality is the soul of business." In some cultures it is a matter of profound respect and education. Therefore be punctual! In doing so, you will be at least showing respect for the person or group of people you are about to meet. As is widely known, respect is something that everyone deserves.

<u>*Tone of voice*</u>

Learn how to speak with a pleasant tone of voice. Once again, ask your friends or relatives for a sincere opinion concerning this aspect, and if needed try to work on it.

I know an investor who prior to investing in a new company would first call in to listen to the voice of the secretary or anyone else answering the phone. Based on that impression he decided to invest or not, because in his opinion if the tone of voice of the person attending the company's phone would strike the clients as unpleasant they might just be turned off. In fact, this notion is confirmed by Susan Ward, creator of the Blog "Small business: Canada guide."[1] According to her, the phone is still the first meeting point between client and company. So, in most cases, clients will have their first impression of the company based on how the phone calls are answered.[2]

Neat appearance, wearing appropriate attire, and obviously coming on time (I stress again: punctual!), you will stand a good chance to cause a good impression. But, this is not everything! You must be able to cope and perform the task on hand. Vic Mignogna (American singer) once said: "your connections may bring you to the door, but they won't keep you there!" Therefore, prepare yourself not only to cause a good impression, but to perform at the level expected of you.

_<u>Preparation</u>_

No matter what type of meeting you are going to attend, it is imperative to have an idea of what is expected from you. Before a meeting, interview or a presentation, get informed about the objective of that particular event. Try to find out the subject of the meeting, who will join, what do they do and what are their interests, and the most important of all, as I mentioned before, what is expected from you. Obviously this is not always an easy task, but you must do your homework before attending the meeting. The better prepared you are for a meeting, the easier it is to cause a good impression and to obtain what you want.

Internet, doubtlessly, is an excellent tool, and it can be of great help for your preparation.

I am frequently joined in meetings by others entrepreneurs, CEOs and scientists, and it is very common to exchange emails before arranging a meeting. An obvious way to find out who will join the meeting is to check the list of people who got copies of the emails. From these email addresses it is possible to extract information about them.

What you must also do before a business meeting is to get informed as much as possible about the company. Read all you can about it! Get informed about its products, areas of work, the history, as well as the profile of the management team, specially of those from the department you are interested in. Read articles written by them. The more you know, the better off you will be.

It is very likely, that you will have to make public presentations such as a seminar in a conference or a speech about a product or even a Master or PhD thesis defense. What to do in such events? As in the case of an interview, the secret for the success of the presentation is preparation! Even if you consider yourself an excellent public speaker and a specialist in that subject, get prepared for the presentation!

Few weeks prior my PhD defense, I had the opportunity to practice my final presentation. My friends and colleagues were my public. I presented that umpteen times, each time to a different friend or colleague. To each one of them I asked to raise questions about what they might not have understood (some of them had no clue about nanotecnology or physical chemistry, what forced me develop the ability to explain complex subjects with simple words), or to mention points that, in their opinion could be asked by the professors on the actual defense. I also asked them to give me a feedback about the way I presented the matter as well as about the work itself.

Those "rehearsals" were decisive for the success of my final presentation, since my friends had asked me questions about things that I had never thought before or things that I didn't consider important, but were actually asked during the real test.

On the day of my defense, I noticed that, every time a professor asked me a question about something, that I had discussed before with one of my friends, the answer flowed smoothly and naturally. However, when questions were made about particularities that I hadn't thought about before, I had to concentrate quite a lot in order to find the right answer. Given that concentration means energy expending, my energy level was dropping along with the unexpected questions. In this process, the ability to concentrate also decreases making it harder to find the next right answer. Therefore, once again, prepare yourself!

Either in a job interview or in a PhD defense or even in a meeting to raise money or solicit the support for a project, you must have in mind, that your interviewer is not there to help or to give advice, but to judge you! In a job interview, for example, the interviewer must be convinced that you are the best candidate for that position. He has no guaranty that you will be an excellent professional. He must look for criteria to judge whether you are or are not the right person. His opinion about you will be formed on the basis of your CV, your answers during the interview, your letters of recommendation, your body language and how you dress. If any of these criteria gives him an unfavorable impression he will use that against you.

We are constantly tested by others, if you know where you will be tested, it becomes easier to succeed! The first impression is therefore decisive and equips us with the safe-conduct to pass the different tests we are submitted to on regular basis henceforth.

A Few years ago I had the privilege of meeting Ruben Dias, founder and CEO of Leading Capital, a Portuguese investment company which is active not only in Portugal but in other European countries as well as in North America.

Ruben analyses projects and supervises the development of companies he invests in. He appears very often in meetings with new potential entrepreneurs who are looking for investment for their projects; or interviewing people who will manage some of his investments.

For someone like Ruben, is practically impossible or at least very risky to take too long to make a decision about a new project or person. In many cases, due to the nature of his work, he must make an impromptu decision based on his first impression. I addressed Ruben on this subject and I feel you can also learn quite a bit from the interview he had granted me cited below.

**How important is the first impression in the business world? What are the critical points that every new entrepreneur should observe to cause a good first impression?**

**Ruben:** "There is never a second chance to cause a good impression", that's a common phrase that we hear in business. I have read from reliable sources that we generally make up our opinion about somebody during the first 45 seconds of our first acquaintance. A simple example of a way to risk a good impression is to arrive late at a meeting. The worst way to start a meeting is to say : "I'm sorry, for being late." Starting to be sorry is not a good way to cause a good impression.

Having been an entrepreneur for more than 18 years, I have found that we can generally cause a good impression if we abide by three imperatives: empathy for the other, clear understanding of what we want to achieve (being objective and to the point) and interest in and a willing to learn from the other person. If I want to cause a good impression, I plan ahead.

Before an important meeting, any type of negotiation or relevant business encounter, I ask myself the question: "what do I want to achieve?", "what outcome would serve my purpose?" I then ask myself the same question of what would satisfy the other party and concentrate on being objective on my first encounter. People like to have a clear understanding of what you want to achieve. They also like to talk about what motivates them, so I have learned that it is better to listen than to talk. A side benefit is that we always learn something from somebody. Several years ago, I wanted to engage in a strategic partnership with Microsoft Portugal. At the time, we were still a very small company so achieving a strategic partnership with Microsoft seemed almost impossible. On my first meeting with the Marketing Director he started to talk about something that he was very enthusiastic about: a restaurant business he was running with his wife. I recall that I asked a lot of questions about his passion and he talked for more than two hours! At the end of the meeting he was so thrilled that he said, "great, let's go ahead with this partnership!" which we hardly talked about...

**What to do in case we caused a bad impression in the first meeting or interview? What is the best way to revert this situation? Is it possible to overcome a "bad first impression"?**

**Ruben:** A bad impression is generally the outcome of a poorly planned meeting. If we are sloppy and disorganized or misleading on a first encounter, it is very difficult, not to say impossible to turn around the other person´s opinion. Communicating clearly, sincerely and with empathy, is a good mix for success. I don´t like the word impossible because there is usually a "way out", although it can be a tough challenge. From my experience, reversing a first bad impression is possible by admitting that you haven´t made the best impression and getting back on track to the success formula.

**By now we are fully aware how important the first impression is, but, despite having achieved that goal, you can also be trapped into the wrong kind of conclusions. Did you misjudge a particular person or project resulting from your 'first impression' experience?**

**Ruben:** I would say that I have always got the better end in every business deal. I have either gained money or gained experience... I have made some mistakes from a first impression judgment. I am very positive in life so I always try to find the good things from a overall bad experience. If you are willing to learn from your mistakes, you are always a winner!

The first impression is influenced, and in some cases, determined by our gut feeling, usually based on previous experiences. When people ask us why we don't like someone or a particular product, sometimes the answer is just: "I don't know, but I have a bad feeling about it!" Is such a "feeling" worth anything? In his book, "The New Leaders"[3], Daniel Goleman speaks about the relevance of gut feelings while making decisions. He explains that while a leader executes his daily work, making decisions, judging situations and observing the results of his decisions, the brain organizes and automatically associates such decisions with the results. Doing so, the brain learns and stores, subconsciously, the rules underlying the decisions that were used in the events, as the leader accumulates knowledge from the practical experiences of life.

Still according to Daniel Goleman, when we face a moment when the decision rules are needed, the brain silently applies them to obtain the best result. Consequently, the brain won't inform us verbalizing the decision, but the emotive part of the brain activates the circuitry that go from the limbic centers into the gut, given us the gratifying feeling that "this is right."

An investor will not invest in a new project if he has a bad feeling about what it, even if he can't rationally explain for rejecting it, since this feeling (or intuition) is simply based on life-long experiences. The same principle can be applied to a job interview.

When we enter an office or a meeting room, our senses capture all information data, such as sounds, images, smells, etc. and create associations with previous sensations. Then we draw conclusions! Therefore it is imperative to understand that the first impression is very important for the success of any project.


*"You never get a second chance to make a first impression"*
Anonymous

# 5. Global x local

In October 2009 I saw in Toronto, a marketing campaign, organized by the Toronto Business Association (TABIA), entitled "Support your neighborhood business! – Think Big – Buy Local."[1]

Why should I buy in the little store of my neighborhood, while I could go shopping in the big downtown supermarket? Does it make sense to focus on "small" and local things, while I can get much more from "big" and global ones? The answer to this question is rather simple: Yes, it makes sense to focus on "small" things.

It is very important to observe our "micro" environment, since there, we can test our ideas and so learn loads of things, which will become a solid groundwork for our projects and will encourage us to take larger steps.

Anyone who desires to become a leader must see his work as having global proportions, but initially acting locally.

To think big, with global proportions, is not a problem, but not starting locally is a mistake.

A local action is not only limited to commercialize your products with your neighbors. It is important to get the community involved with your project, so they will become supporters of your idea.

Let's suppose you dream about becoming a famous musician, already imagining tours around the globe or degrees from famous universities, but you continuously neglect the opportunities to perform at your local school, you will have little chances to step on other stages.

Your neighbors, relatives and friends must be considered as your first and most valuable fans or clients.

Observing Joseph's story we can clearly see that he took very seriously the local aspect, when he first met Pharaoh.

In order to face the approaching crisis, Joseph presents an "emergency economic plan." It would be needed seven years of hard work, during the "fat cows" period, for the country to accumulate enough wealth to overcome the seven following years of hardship. Joseph suggests in his plan that all the grains, which were to be produced, should be stored in the cities, where the work was done.

Joseph's idea of keeping the grains in the local warehouses, not only decentralized the work, but also reduced potential tensions with local leaders, and at the same time, made the future distribution of food less complicated. Giving the local leaders the responsibility over this project made them and the others involved with the work, feel important and brought prosperity to their own villages.

Since there was no need to transport the grains over large distances, Joseph was also reducing costs and the typical losses of grains due to transportation. It is well known that, even with all the technology we have today and paved roads, between one and two percent of grains are lost during transportation.[2]

Other important and interesting factor to consider a local action is the opportunity to convince first the people who are nearest to you. When you start a new business endeavor, but you can't convince your family, friends or colleagues to invest in it or to support it, you will have little chances to convince the others who don't know you.

Most venture investors do not invest in a project, which was not yet tested at a local level or at a small scale, no matter how convincing the idea sounds like. Obviously it is a good thing to have dreams with global proportions, but it is very important to test them at a small scale first. It doesn't mean that your dream won't work at the global level, just because it failed locally; however your chances to have a global success are quite small when the local was a failure.

A local project is easier to control and to restructure if needed, since there are fewer variables. Moreover when we learn from our mistakes at local level we will be better prepared to face the global challenges.

In 2008 I had the pleasure to meet Agnus Proksch, a German born in Romania, who graduated in Nutrition Science and Home Economics, who had recently returned from Kenya, after an unsuccessful entrepreneurial experience to establish a dried fruits company in the heart of Africa. I had the opportunity to talk to him about his experience and about the reasons that caused the collapse of this idea. You can see in this interview that neglecting the "local" can cost the "global."

**How did the idea of a dried fruits company in Africa start?**

**Agnus:** it started by someone who was already reselling dried fruits here in Europe. He wanted to start in Kenya because he was getting the dried fruits from some countries in Africa, but when there were complains, he couldn't do much, because he was just the reseller. Therefore he wanted to start his own company to have a better control over the material and the production.

**How big was the dream?**

**Agnus:** He wanted to have a factory to produce 200 tons/year. Out of 10 kg of pineapple you make 1 kg of dried pineapple. It means we would need 2000 tons of pineapple per year to produce 200 tons. Take in account that we wanted to do everything with organic certification. The idea was sound, since we could make a lot of money, since in some cases the end price for dried pineapples can be up to 30 Euros/kg.

**Why didn't work?**

**Agnus:** When I got to Kenya to implement the project, I found some issues:

First, the certification was not in place! You need at least a year to get the organic certification. We couldn't sell anything.

Secondly, we had an African partner, who was suppose to help me, since I was the CEO, but he was not informing me of everything, moreover he also demanded more money than we could pay him. He was important, because he knew the language and had the contacts. But I had to implement a project without his help. So I had to hire another one who was living there and also had contact with the farmers.

Thirdly, the founders of the company wanted organic certified pineapples to sell to Europe right away, but we didn't have the infrastructure.

And finally there was no marketing done to commercialize the fruits in Africa for example.

**Did you get enough pineapples?**

**Agnus:** After a year of work, we sent a 12 ton container, but they could not sell anything. Because I was told that half of the fruits did not arrive in a state that could be sold. So I was blamed for everything.

**How valuable would have been to test initially the idea inside Africa?**

**Agnus:** We were too fixed in exporting! We should have sold in the local market first. We could have started a relationship with the farmers. The farmers believe in what they see, they don't believe in what you say. They even told me that they would sell me the pineapples, but once I was there, they wouldn't have the fruits, because they had already sold to smaller local dealers, coming with their bikes. We were seen as the people who were coming to take their "bread." We thought that we were helping the farmers, but the locals didn't see this way. But I never noticed that, and my own workers never told me that there was a relationship problem. So my containers were empty. If we were doing business there first, we could meanwhile buy a chamber to mimic the conditions in a container, thus we would do the normal steps to test if we were already able to export. We believed that the fruits would arrive in good conditions in Europe without testing the hypothesis, but that would have meant some investment too.

**Why didn't you start selling locally?**

**Agnus:** Because we were too focused to export!

**When did you realize that this business model was not going to work?**

**Agnus:** After a year and two months, we noticed this! We had our own internal crises! We never thought about failure! We just didn't consider this possibility, so we were not ready for that.

I told the shareholders that the whole thing wouldn't work! We had to restart, but this time "small."

**What did they say?**

**Agnus:** They said it would not be worth starting small! They would rather loose the invested money than to invest in a small business! They considered the profit to be too small.

**Do you believe starting "small" would have worked?**

**Agnus:** First of all, we should have planned how much we could spend. We didn't even have a clear budget, how did the shareholders expected us to run a big company?

Secondly, we should have shown the local people that we wanted to be a partner, that we were a serious partner and that they could rely on us. We were not managing to be a good business partner with the locals, the way they understand business.

Thirdly, we were too dependent on them! We should have hired some of them to grow the pineapples for ourselves, to have our own production. It takes 2 years to grow pineapples. This also shows commitment to the place, because people would see that you were not going to leave any moment. This happened before; someone started a project and left so the farmers were very skeptical!

The farmers were afraid that we would leave any time, so they wouldn't invest a lot to increase their production, because they had no guaranty we would stay there. We were competing against the local consumers, who were for sure coming back to buy the farmers' fruits.

**Do you think that after two years the business would have grown?**

**Agnus:** Yes, the same pineapple roots would work up to 10 years, so we would have our own fruit production. And we could buy the fruits from the farmers as well. Moreover the farmers would follow the technologies that we would have implemented. They need these practical things in order to make the thing work. It is not enough to tell them about a vision, you must bring it to reality.

**Was there any other local service or product that you were neglecting?**

**Agnus:** Not really! But the relationship with the farmers was critical.

**Were there other particularities that caused problems?**

**Agnus:** Yes, for example we wanted to buy a piece of land, but there was a dispute between two tribes, which delayed the whole process. This happened during elections. We were living in a territory from a tribe, but we bought the land from someone who, although living there, he was not a local, but from another tribe. This was a problem, which we didn't know in the beginning.

Little things were causing trouble too. For example, there was no company there that produced proper boxes for pineapples. We didn't think about that before, so we had to produce our own boxes.

Besides these little problems, one of the hardest things to get used to is the fact that they (the locals) say one thing, but it means something else, because the culture is very different. You must understand the body language!

They can agree with their mouth about the price, but in their brains they didn't agree and they won't do business. In Africa people usually don't say NO! It is in general rude to say no to people that you don't know. They won't tell you, but you should understand.

Who could have imagined that the apparent lack of compromise with the local farmers would literally rotten the plans to build up a multimillion company? Obviously this was not the only reason for the downfall of the company, but from this experience it is clear that understanding the local culture is indispensable for success. It is very important to obtain the support of the "small."

To ignore the "details" can be fatal for any project. Great world powers lost wars against "tiny" nations, just because neglected or were unaware of the local aspects.

A careful observation and a good knowledge of the local potentials were the keys for Muhammad Yunus to found the Grameen bank, in Bangladesh. The use of microcredit for poor people to be able to create their own businesses, escaping then from poverty, was a revolutionary idea, which in 2006, granted to Muhammad Yunus and to his bank, the Nobel Peace Price[3].

In an article published by the Havard Business School, the professors Christopher Marquis and Julie Battilana emphasize that "despite globalization, local factors remain important, and in many ways local particularities have become more visible and salient as globalization has proceeded."[4]

In a study about small business in the US, it was shown that for each $100.00 spent in a "global" company, only $12.00 reverted in benefits to the local community, while from the $100.00 placed in a local company, $45.00 reverted to the benefit of the local community.[5]

Such factors obviously cause an impact in the minds of those, who can become supporters of any project.

A common error of new entrepreneurs, right in the beginning of their businesses is to open a bank account in a multinational bank, thinking this will facilitate their international businesses. However, once the first financial problems occur, they see the mistake they made. When they try to negotiate debts or to ask for advanced payments; they must listen to answers such as "sorry, we can't decide it here, but in the headquarters!" And the problem takes a long time to be solved, if ever. The ideal case is to look for a local bank, where you have more chances to meet the people who can indeed make decisions, who will definitely help you quickly.

As much as possible, choose for your company or project, a local marketing team, an Internet provider and other services. Doing so, you strengthen the bonds between your project and the local community. People around will recognize the value of your actions and they will observe the direct impact in their communities. They quickly become your supporters. Besides that, you probably reduce costs. You must however abdicate the use of local services or products if they compromise the quality of your project or product.

In my district, there is a supermarket from a big national chain, full of all sort of goods; a great variety of fruits and vegetables, a bakery, large shelves with dairy products, and clothes, and cleaning products. This supermarket is open until 9 pm from Monday to Saturday. Every week I receive in my mailbox their advertising. But what got my attention those days was the fact that 10 meters away from this giant supermarket, there is a grocery store that doesn't even have a name; it offers only few foodstuffs; it has only one employee (the owner!) and it closes at 6 pm. While I was watching "David" just 10 meters away from "Goliath", I asked myself: "How could this grocery store survive under these conditions?" Then I noticed it was hard to see the products through the shop windows, because they were covered with announcements from the activities that happen in our district:

- The pupils from the school X are inviting everyone for a beneficent concert...

- The dancing group will meet this week at the following address...

- Now you can learn Capoeira at...

There you go! This simple connection between that grocery store and the local community was the secret for the survival of that business!

Even with the possibility of buying at the supermarket with a great variety of products and sales, some locals decided to be faithful clients of the grocery store, because they identified themselves with it; they felt that store was part of their community, family-like.

To think "small" is important for new entrepreneurs and young politicians as well as for those who are looking for supporters for projects or looking for a job.

An organic growth of any project can be only achieved by observing and respecting the local aspects.

*"A local company has more accountability"*
*Paul Hawken*

 # 6. Gathering information

Dr. House[1] used to say "patients lie!" The only problem is that they lie as much as doctors, professors, lawyers and the like.

We must accept the sad reality that "people tell lies!" According to Dr. Robert Feldman, professor of psychology and author of the book "The liar in your life." Two people getting acquainted, lie to each other an average of three times in ten minutes.[2]

How then to find truth in the middle of this pile of lies that we receive everyday?

To find the truth is not only the duty of police officers, investigators, journalists or people from other related professions. In any field of work, the truth (no matter what it represents) comes mixed with lies in all sorts of shape. To be successful in our profession as in our life, we must develop the ability to distinguish true information from false.

As it was discussed in chapter two, body language is an indispensable tool to find out, without words, what is really happening around us, but the most common way to find detailed information is an interview, which is one of the oldest procedures to obtain information.

It is important to understand that in the search for information, interviewing is an investigative tool and therefore, for better results, should not be used alone, but together with other tools such as document analysis, body language, etc.

No matter if you are looking for a job, or working for a company, where your role is to select the best candidate for a job vacancy, or even if you are trying to discover how to convince a potential client, you may need to turn to an interview to achieve your goals.

Remember that a casual conversation can be turned into a very effective interview, but for that, you must be able to let the interviewees feel comfortable to speak with you, to open their hearts, to freely express themselves about the subject. This is the reason why basically most interviewers start an interview with an "easy" subject to break the ice. In doing so, you will let the other person feel relaxed, making it easier for communication to happen effectively.

Although it may sound obvious (for many interviewers is not!), it is important to highlight that you must let the other person speak! Even if you know the answer to the question, be patient and let the person speak.

It is not useful as an interviewer to appear as if you know it all, therefore avoid showing your own knowledge, but let the interviewee feel in the position of an "expert", very comfortable to speak about the subject.

We all have the tendency to keep quite before an expert. The expert's "aura" may inhibit people from expressing their thoughts. In such situations most people, if not all, feel afraid to give an opinion about any subject, since we are facing an "authority." Most people feel afraid to say something trivial or even wrong and to look like fools.

In the book "Start with No"[4], the author encourages the "interviewers", while in a business meeting, to look like "beginners" or to show some "fragility", thus the other people will feel comfortable giving their opinions and to freely expressing themselves and to speak a lot, potentially revealing important information that could be useful to make decisions.

Observing the meeting between Joseph and his brothers you can see the technique he used to obtain valuable information. Joseph had a leadership position; this alone was enough to inhibit anyone who would come close to him. Anyone who had to talk to him would be very careful with his words.

When he saw his brothers coming, he preferred not to reveal himself, since that moment wouldn't have been the right time. Given that it was very important for him to discover whether his brothers had abandoned their violent and envious nature or not, if he had revealed himself that moment he wouldn't have had the opportunity to discover it. He then used a very clever method to obtain the truth about his brothers.

First of all, he called an interpreter to be between him and his brothers, which in his brothers' eyes, put him in a lower position, since he wouldn't be able to speak their language or to understand them. This fact also made his bothers feel comfortable speaking amongst themselves in their own language. Secondly, when he accused his brothers of espionage, he made them speak. He didn't make their lives easy, and for each explanation from his brothers, he would insist he didn't believe them. Every time his brothers tried to convince Joseph that they were innocent, they released more personal information that Joseph could use to to judge whether they were trustworthy or not.

Initially, Joseph obtained the following information from his brothers: We are all brothers. Children from the same father. We are here to buy food. He knew all that, so continued applying the tactics of "I don't believe!" to learn more. Then he hears "we are twelve brothers from Canaan, the youngest stayed with the father and one of the brothers died."

So far the information he collected was true, but not enough to know if the brothers had indeed changed and were finally trustworthy. However to use the same tactics of not believing in them, wouldn't be enough and it could even be counterproductive, since his brothers could just give up trying to convince him. Joseph then changed the strategy to gain more time in order to obtain more detailed information. It was important for Joseph to hear his brothers speaking about the events that happened many years ago, of when they betrayed and sold him.

He insisted that he didn't believe; however this time, he didn't want explanations, but demanded actions. He decided to keep one of the brothers in Egypt, while the others would travel back home to bring the youngest brother, Benjamin, to Egypt. It was important to Joseph to see that his younger brother Benjamin was alive. That would help Joseph to trust again in his brothers.

It wouldn't be an easy task to bring Benjamin to Egypt, and this was troubling the brothers. However, in the presence of Joseph they felt comfortable to speak about this issue in their own language, since they supposed that Joseph didn't understand them, given that he used an interpreter to communicate with them. This became a very relevant moment in that meeting. The brothers talk among themselves, revealing that they felt guilty for everything that had happened in the past, and they believed that they were being punished for the crime they committed long ago against their brother Joseph.

If we pay attention to Joseph's story, we can learn a very valuable lesson. Only through a slow and meticulous process it is possible to obtain important information that will be useful to make right decisions.

Police officers, Investigators, Special Agents, Lawyers, Journalists in their search for important and trustworthy information, usually exercise this method of insisting that they are not convinced about what they hear or asking the same question but with different words, looking for contradictions.

Another intelligent method to be used in an interview, is the so called "silence approach", very common among TV hosts, who create the "silence" to force the interviewees to provide more information, since silence in such situations bring about discomfort, pushing interviewees to speak.

A good interview demands talent and preparation.

In 2002 I met Dulce Neto, a Portuguese Journalist, who was an editor of one of the most prestigious newspapers from Portugal. Thanks to her talent she overcame many barriers to become successful in her profession. I talked to her about her secrets to find truth through an interview.

**What is the difference between a good and a mediocre journalist?**

**Dulce:** The good journalist:

1) Does the homework, before asking questions;

1) Investigates the subject or gets information about the person he will write about;

2) Knows how to ask questions and he is not afraid to ask them;

3) Knows how to choose the important or interesting information;

4) Knows how to structure a text, which will catch the attention of those who read it or listen to it. Knows how to tell a story, without interfering with the story;

5) Confirms the information he received;

6) Looks for the other side of the coin. If you say I hit you, the journalist must listen to my version;

7) Respects the 'out of records' and never reveals who the source is.

**Some interviewers use the silence, others repeat the same question looking for contradictions. What is in your your opinion the best method to find the truth?**

**Dulce:** This depends on the interviewee and on the media the journalist is working for. The bottom line is that it varies from a seduction style to a more aggressive one. In the written media or even recorded work (TV and Radio recorded shows), which are not live and have other timings, there are two ways: One is to leave the difficult questions to the end, making the interviewees feel comfortable, then creating empathy gaining trust, and finally asking the questions we know are troublesome. It is worthwhile showing that you know something of what you are looking for, to "deceive" him a little bit, which makes him think we already know something resulting in him opening up. The second method, which is not exclusive and can or must be used together with the first is quit the inconvenient question, but ask it again later to find out any contradictions.

When we have a live program, then the situation gets complicated; we have little time, so the best thing to do is to go directly to the questions you have to ask. Be straightforward and don't give up, confronting what the interviewee says with the data he doesn't have. Be clear, to the point: "You are not answering my question!" It doesn't always work. Often you waste time, the person just answers with excuses. The journalist wastes time and can only show that the interviewee doesn't want to answer. You just can't get an answer. So don't waste your time, but try to use the first approach and ask the same question later using different words, trying to find contradictions.

**What can we do, when we know the interviewee is a "professional liar"?**

**Dulce:** To try to catch him in his lies. Do not believe in what he says. Do not write anything down unless it is confirmed. Compare everything he says with other sources. It all depends on the objective you may have; if it is an interview that will be just published without any further research or if it is to be used as a source of information. If it is the first case and we still decide to interview such a person (which is rare, since we usually avoid such individuals), one must, along with the questions, try to find out the contradictions, to show to the reader or listener, that that person is no reliable. If it is the second case, and you want to use the

114

interview as a source of information, then you must listen to everything and compare it with documents and other sources, publishing only that which has been confirmed (if the person wants to remain anonymous) or together with the other opinions (if the person agrees to be identified).

### How do you know if the person is lying?

**Dulce:** Often we don't know. Once again it depends on the subject and on the person you are interviewing. If you are well prepared (if it was possible to be prepared), you will notice the lies, because you see that the data don't match together. Sometimes we notice only afterwards, when we check the information

### Are people afraid of journalists?

**Dulce:** Yes!

### Why?

**Dulce:** Several reasons, all connected to one thing: The journalist is just a medium, not the end. Whatever they say will reach the masses, it will be public, and so people get exposed. To a greater or lesser degree, the interviewee exposes himself, even if he doesn't say anything, or refuses to speak; since the journalist can just say that "the person refused to speak about the subject." Silence, with a name, has a value. Whoever reads the text will form an opinion; "he doesn't want to speak, because he is afraid", "he doesn't want to speak because he doesn't know", "because he doesn't respect the media and the rights to information", "he doesn't want to speak because he doesn't trust in that newspaper", "he doesn't want to speak because he has the rights to and he'd better be quiet ", etc.

A journalist is a medium that you can't control. Neither what he says nor how he says. He is not a machine. He is a person, and even if he is a good professional and abides to the rules and ethics, he is subjective. So, he will choose what he wants from the information he obtains from the interviewee, and will publish what he judges important, although he is trying to be objective. Therefore many people try to read what the journalist wrote, before it is published. As a rule, a journalist should not allow his text to be read before being published. You either trust or you don't... Otherwise the text could be modified according to the interviewees' will.

Journalists have power, which is not easily controllable, especially if they are good professional. It is not simple to talk to a journalist. They may make us say things that we didn't want to say that way. It can also happen that you don't know how to express yourself well and deliver a message wrongly. Many people, after they say something, they just don't admit they said that. It is a common practice to show a recording of the interview for the person to admit that he said what was published.

You must also consider the fact that, in some cases, the journalist may gain the trust and empathy of the interviewee, so that the person forgets he is before a professional who is at work and not a friend, to whom he would tell things, not wishing that they would become public. In some cases, an honest journalist noticing the situation, would ask "do you really want to say that?" or the interviewee may notice he was too far and says, "Please, this is off the record!" (the journalist shouldn't publish it!); or in the worst cases, it is just a way to release lies, since the interviewee says "you can write this, but don't put my name on it..."

Finally, there is the genuine fear from bad journalism. Bad professionals, who twist what was said, who decontextualize, who invent things, etc. And it is very hard to efficiently contradict some untruth that has become public.

Summarizing then, people are afraid of journalists, because they know that this is a power, which they can't control. This power is getting weaker everyday however, because of the Internet, since people no longer need a mediator or a medium.

For obvious reasons, Joseph didn't trust in his brothers. Only through an intelligent use of interviews was it possible to trust in them again, and finally rebuild the bonds that had been broken in the past.

For an investigator or a journalist, the discovery of truth is crucial, because this is the driving force to propel a project, career, or any other personal enterprise. For Joseph, it was the best way to give him back his inner peace and his family.

We all, at any one time, will have to face a situation, where we must judge other people, places, opinions, information, ideas, etc. in order to discover what we consider important, or the truth. Learning how to interview is one of basic steps to find what we are looking for.

*"Silence is a source of great strength"*
Lao Tzu

7. Never give up!

*"... For God has caused me to be fruitful in the land of my affliction."*
*Genesis 41:52*

Betrayed by his brothers, sold as a slave and arrested unjustly, Joseph had all reasons to give up dreaming! All knowledge, talents, experience and networking would be worth nothing if Joseph had not mustered perseverance.

William E. Jennings conducted a study entitled "A profile of the Entrepreneur"[1], and he listed the seven most important characteristics for success with **perseverance** in first place! The world is full of noteworthy examples of perseverance.

The young Walt Disney, for example, was fired from his work at the Kansas City Star newspaper because his boss considered him lacking creativity. Following this first failure, Disney founded the company Laugh-O-Gram Films which soon bankrupted and left him in such a dismal situation that he almost couldn't pay his rent anymore. He still suffered other failures before reaching success.[2]

What about Thomas Edison, in his indefatigable fight for developing the electric lamp?

Joseph, Disney, Edison and many others would not have accomplished their dreams if they had not been persistent.

Everyday many people around the globe abandon their dreams, giving up, in most cases, at the first obstacles, losing the battle right at the beginning. They failed to persevere.

The most common barrier and probably the number one reason for the smashing of most dreams is a simple word "no". "My boss said my project is 'not' interesting", "the marketing team said 'no' to my idea!", "I was told I had 'no' talent!"

We should interpret the word "no" only as a sign, not as an insurmountable obstacle. Everyone who achieved professional success, no doubt, came across the word "no" along his career but made it to the top nonetheless. If "no" is a word that frequently crosses your way, you should rethink your plans, look for new roads, but never give up.

I personally don't know of any business enterprise, academic research project or any other endeavor for that matter which had set out and reached success without being compelled to alter its initial plans and intentions. Basically, all projects go through reevaluations, reformulations and, in some cases, radical changes, given that not all methods and ideas will work as initially conceived. Therefore, you must be ready and willing to alter some of your initial thoughts in order to reach your goals.

In the book "Getting to plan B"[3] the authors show that most famous companies reached success with a plan B (sometimes C, D or even Z), in other words, something different from initial conception. Thus Google, Starbucks, Pay Pal and many others wouldn't be what they are today if they had stuck to the original plan.

It is during moments of frustration and change where perseverance mainly comes into play. This was one of Joseph's outstanding attributes, and surely the most meritorious characteristic of winners.

It is, however, important to have a balance (what is not easy!) between persistence and the ability to notice when something proves unworkable, in line with an old saying "if the horse you are riding drops dead, it's a good time to dismount." This usually applies to the methods one uses to accomplish the dreams, not to the dream itself.

Joseph literally had reached rock bottom being imprisoned, but didn't allow his brain to be imprisoned. He didn't give up but persevered to achieve what he was dreaming about.

In my third year at university I tried to apply for a traineeship in a company. Although being friendly, the owner of the company rejected me by saying 'no'. These two letters were enough to dismantle all my plans concerning that company, and, worst of all, made me give up looking for other traineeships in other companies. I just didn't imagine that receiving a 'no' would be the most common thing in my professional life. It is nothing unusual to hear a 'no' again and again.

When we founded our first company in Toronto, Smart Biotech, I was responsible to contact investors and convincing them to read our business plan.

Investors, especially in the venture capital world, receive many business plans everyday. Working your way through a pile of papers is not an easy task. Therefore, it is important to put a voice or a face behind the document. So, making a brief phone call before sending the business plan is a very effective marketing tool. But before reckoning with a potential "no" from the investor I had to anticipate the potential "no" of his secretary.

Secretaries are trained to "filter" phone calls, letting only the important calls to be transferred to the boss. Some secretaries are well trained to say "no!" I had to develop my own strategy of reducing the probability of receiving a no from the secretaries. In case you are facing the same situation here is the formula:

1) Call in the morning (for whatever reason, this makes a big difference!);

2) Speak with a pleasant tone of voice and be very courteous;

3) Introduce yourself by your surname: "Hi, this is Dr. Montenegro" and try to establish some sort of intimacy with the person you are trying to contact, saying for example, "How is Joseph today?"

4) Then mention that you need her help to contact the person (boss, investor, producer, etc.)

If she is still not convinced to put you through but asks you to leave a message, then you must parry in a different way:

5)      Very calmly, explain your project using very complicated words (the more complex, the better), asking her to pass the message to her boss. If she is confused or uncertain about delivering the correct message, she will, in all likelihood, ask her boss again if he has some minutes to talk to you.

If, however, you chance to talk to a secretary with a PhD in Physics then your really last resource is to call again the next day and ask if she handed over the message and if her boss would have some minutes to talk to you.

There are plenty of barriers in the professional world, the competition is fierce, the pace is intense, there are just a few opportunities and sometimes we pay a very high price for our blunders. However, such drawbacks are not spared in anybody's life, they are a fact in most people's professional lives. Perseverance has, in most cases, made the difference between winners and losers!

In 2005 I had the pleasure to meet Don MacAdams, an American living in Canada, who founded MBVAX, a company that develops a vaccine against cancer. Since this vaccine doesn't conform with the typical methods of the big pharmaceutical companies, he faces a gigantic fight. But for someone who went through many ups and downs of professional life, no barriers will stop him. Witness the following interview:

**How many times did you hit the bottom and had to start again?**

**Don:** Three!

**What was your biggest business failure as well as your biggest achievement?**

**Don:** Since "Business" to my mind has to do with money, I must admit my "biggest business failure" was one of the better things I have done, and the "biggest achievement" one of the worst. From an early age I knew how to chase a buck, and by my thirties my buck-chasing abilities had been hone to Olympian proportions. I made bundles of money when I took Varah Electronics my first company public (to the stock exchange market) in 1984 at age 37, and rightfully took my place as a member of the Canadian aristocracy. I bought the Firestone Estate, nine thousand square feet of luxury with seven fenced acres on the brow of the Ancaster escarpment. I had a blue Mercedes SEL, an art collection including an original Modigliani drawing of Guillaume Apollinaire and an oil attributed to J. M. W. Turner, a collection of medieval manuscripts including the largest group of English manorial court documents in Canada, a collection of rare books including a first edition of Dicken's Bleak House, a wine cellar of classified Bordeaux and sixty-year-old Armagnac, and a fierce Rottweiler to protect it all. I had all of these things and the lifestyle to go along with them including European vacations via the QE2 and Concorde, suites at the Old England in Windermere, the Ritz in London, the Grand in Paris, the Intercontinental in Geneva, the Meridian in Nice, and other fine hotels everywhere in between. My wife had the finest clothes, furs and jewelry, and my kids had way more than any other kids including a new Mustang convertible for my daughter on the Christmas following her sixteenth birthday. However, I was not happy.

Just before my 40$^{th}$ birthday, I sold my company and spent a month solo trekking in Nepal. When I returned from that trip, I started Annulus Technical Industries to manufacture a high density electronic switch I had recently patented. I loved this company and worked like never before – I learned mechanical engineering and built the tooling and production equipment with my own hands. But the company was a big drain on cash and eventually I had to dispose of my possessions to pay for it. The big house lasted five years. I downsized everything and moved my business and home to the small fishing village of Port Dover. Annulus continued its downward spiral and I eventually had to close it down for good in 1993. But I was happy.

**Why did you fail?**

**Don:** Technology is a treadmill. State-of-the-art products become obsolete; it is only a matter of time.

**What is easier to cope with: failure or success?**

**Don:** A successful business if much easier to manage than a failure.

**Is there a formula to forget failure and to move on?**

**Don:** Never forget your failures; these are more valuable than successes.

**It is important to be strong and "never give up", but how can I know when it is the time to admit that something is not meant to work?**

**Don:** You never know until it is too late.

**What should we learn from our failures?**

**Don:** Humility.

**Right now you are leading MBVAX in the development of a vaccine to treat cancer patients. You are no only fighting the disease, but the "status quo" of the pharmaceutical companies, as well as the medical community. How to handle that? What did you learn in the past that is helping you today?**

**Don:** I am not sure I am handling it well, but I am happy.

Don MacAdams' story reminds me that in any professional field or project, one must take risks to reach one's goals, but it is important to keep in mind that the possibility of failure is real, it happens more frequently than one expects. Therefore you don't have to feel ashamed about failure, this experience can teach us valuable lessons. You must, however, learn from them, get up again and move on.

Our first company in Toronto proved a complete failure. We had an excellent team, fully engaged with the project; we had even quit our previous jobs to fight for this dream. The idea looked perfect, flawless, and a team which was willing to work hard to make it big. We responded to almost all questions from investors; we were invited to present our idea to some of the most famous investment companies in Canada, but we could not raise the money we needed to implement the project. In one of the last venture companies we visited, the vice-president received us with the following words: "You are looking for money for almost a year, but you didn't make it yet, why should a listen to you?" We answered that we couldn't explain it either (i.e. failing to raise the necessary funds), but after looking at our project he could maybe help us to find an answer. At the end of the presentation we asked him what, in his opinion, was the reason for our unsuccessful search for money. He just replied: "I don't know, but if nobody invested so far it is because there must a problem and I wouldn't invest either!"

As I said before, the possibility of failure is real, but the more realistically you are aware of this possibility, the better prepared you will be if failure knocks at your door. But remember, if you don't try you have already lost the battle!

After this unsuccessful experience with Smart Biotech, and loosing all money, never a lot to begin with, I lost all motivation to be an entrepreneur once more.

At that time, my colleague and Smart Biotech's co-founder, Dr. Thomas Freier, moved back to Germany and with the help of Aspiras[4], he secured investment fund through a program from Hightech Gründerfonds[5] to found a new company developing medical devices.

He, then, invited me to join him and move to Germany to embark on this new business endeavor. I was still trying to recover from my first failure as entrepreneur, so I asked him for a few days to think about his offer. While reflecting that I would have to move once again to another country, I caught myself asking "what if we fail again?"

That same week I was invited for a job interview with a big Canadian-American company producing plastic products. At the end of the interview when everything seemed to be settled that I would soon start working there, I asked the owner: "Have you ever bankrupted?" He looked at me, smiled and said: "Are you kidding? It happened five times already!" I smiled back and said: "Thanks, this was I needed to know!"

So, Thomas and I founded Medovent Corporation in Germany which so far has been successful in the development of innovative medical implants.

It pays to let persistence prevail!

Let me, nevertheless, draw your attention to an ignored, but very important aspect about perseverance.

Perseverance is related to another word scarcely in use nowadays, almost unknown by the general public: *Temperance!* Anyone who achieved success in life needs to display this virtue (at least in some aspects). Temperance is related to self-control, i.e. being able to check your desires, impulses, and emotions so you may achieve something more worthwhile.

Professional athletes are aware of how important it is to stick to a strict diet, regular exercise, repose properly and accordingly, and exercise restraint to gain victory. Temperance is a very intrinsic aspect of perseverance, and, thus, the formula for success.

As a matter of fact, the great leaders of 19th century emphasized temperance as a very crucial virtue. Stephen Covey, in his bestseller "The 7 habits of highly effective people"[6], lists many characteristics that were decisive in the lives of great personalities of the past. Temperance is one of them.

Is it possible to see temperance in Joseph's character? Yes, indeed, it is! Joseph's temperance is shown in his patience to stand firm against all afflictions, without rebelling against his God. It is also clearly revealed in his disposition to start all over again every time he reached bottom.

Furthermore, this virtue may also be observed in Joseph's life when he manifests self-control before his brothers rather than lusting for revenge while they were bowing down before him. But above all, his temperance clearly becomes patent when he was approached his master's wife. At that moment, he might have considered in an affair with Potiphar's wife as a mean to ease his condition as a slave but, instead, he resisted, since he had other plans in mind and he was fully aware of the risks involved in such decisions.

Often we see talented people loosing everything they had and not being able to stand up again, because they never learned how important it is to observe temperance. Some people cannot resist the temptation to quick riches by resorting to fraudulent schemes, only to be subsequently exposed and lose everything again. Joseph decided to do what he knew was right instead of taking a short cut. This also defines temperance.

To be temperate is to be able to renounce a transitory pleasure for something which is still in the future. To control one's greed and agitation, to wake up early, to be strong to say no, to reject some invitations for the benefit of something more important such as health, to develop the capacity to pass an exam, to give a positive example, to lead a group, or maybe even readying yourself for eternal life - these are all manifestations of temperance.

Temperance and perseverance are intrinsically interwoven!

We all would prefer to exert control over our own lives and our future. If, however, we lack the discipline of curbing our own individual appetite, selfish preferences and/or agitation, how shall we manage our future? No chance. We can't win a war, if we are loosing all little daily battles.

In the book, "Temperance", the author writes that "...temperance alone is... the foundation of victories to be conquered."[7] Who is not in the habit of controlling his impulses minimizes his chances for developing perseverance and, hence, future success.

According to Goleman[8] the major challenge for a leader is self-control.

The struggle for professional success is marked by uncertainties, and it is nearly impossible to heed all its parameters. Therefore, it is imperative to at least master what is within your personal control; pay strict attention to aspects that depend on you only, such as being proactive, acquiring communication skills, and, of course displaying temperance, to list but a few.

Most probably your situation doesn't compare to that of the biblical Joseph having been prisoner in Egypt but, all the same, you can't anticipate a way yet to fulfill your professional dreams. Then look around for opportunities, try to find "Pharaoh's butler", who might just turn out to be your neighbor. Develop the art of communication and learn how to obtain information. In essence, be prepared to cause a very good first impression, be patient and never give up.

When Joseph's second son was born, he called him Ephraim, which means *fruitful* and at that moment he declared: "For God has caused me to be fruitful in the land of my affliction." Surely perseverance paid off for him.

Joseph's story offers us the major tools indispensable for success in any field of work. How about emulating his example?

*"God gives the opportunities; success depends upon the used made of them."*
Ellen G. White, (Patriarchs and Prophets)

 Appendix

**Bonus material**

At this moment, many people around the globe are preparing their résumés hoping to find soon their first Job. They describe their skills, courses, languages, conferences that they attended, etc. However, the lack of practical experience may dim all other qualifications, diminishing the chances of finding a job!

You can avoid this problem by starting a traineeship or work before finishing your education. The following list gives some ideas, where and what you can do to obtain experience and to enlarge your network.

I must say that it is very complicated to included several different professions in distinctive groups, because of the interconnection of the different fields of work as well as the potentialities of each individual profession. So, as I tried to simplify this list, I have reduced the amplitude of each individual line of work. As an example, Psychology, in this table, is classified in the medical field, but as we know, medical psychology is just one of the 56 different areas of psychology according to the American Psychology Association (www.apa.org/about/division.html).

As you will also see, some professions could be together with others, but I have decided to put them separated due to some particularities that could be more deeply explored. Therefore examine the whole list, looking for areas that could be interconnected to your profession or field of work, so new ideas could come up.

In case you have a suggestion for this list, I would appreciate your collaboration. Please write an email to:

**info@josephceo.com**

Regardless of the work area, the secret to have a successful professional start is to face seriously any opportunity. Therefore consider the following three points:

1) Finish what you started!
2) Do the best you can!

Ask people around you what is their opinion about your work, be open for criticism and accept suggestions to improve it. The above two points will make an excellent impact on people around you.

But finally:

3) Be proactive!

I just don't know how to emphasize this enough, then I will repeat: Be proactive! Move on without the need of orders. Build up your own future!

It is not easy, to most people, to be proactive. However, you better start developing this virtue as soon as possible. Remember that this is about your professional future.

Some of the suggestions below are rather simple (that was my intention), so that anyone who has not yet started a traineeship or any other professional activity my start without major barriers.

| Profession or field of work | Where can you probably find a traineeship position | Simple ideas to add to your Curriculum Vitae. Example of projects, traineeship, etc. |
|---|---|---|
| Cooking, Nutrition, etc. | Restaurants, clinics, spas, hotels, nursing homes, orphanages, etc. | - Most restaurants are open for interns.<br>- Offer yourself as a volunteer to work in a orphanage, nursing home, prison, or your district school. Try to improve the local service. |
| Performing arts: Music, Drama, Dance, etc. | Theaters, radio and TV stations, movie producers, folklore groups, circus, etc. | - Follow Pat Adams example and bring happiness to those who are suffering. Organize a music, dance or theater group and perform at hospitals, prisons, etc.<br>- Organize presentations of your work at your own school, church or club.<br>- Produce a short film, be creative, put your film on Youtube or send it for competitions.<br>- Some churches have music or theater groups, join them. |
| Plastic arts | Museums, galleries, schools, clubs, etc. | - Offer yourself to help with the local museums or municipality to restore art works.<br>- Look for an opportunity at a |

|  |  | university or in a club to help with organization of art events.<br>- Offer your help to do the design or decoration of a friend's restaurant, store, hotel, etc.<br>- Decorate your friends' parties. |
|---|---|---|
| Design | Any company that develops its own products. Marketing agencies. Web design companies, etc. | - Try to get an intern position in any company that develops its own products: automobiles, clothes, furniture, industrial machines, etc.<br>- Packaging companies are excellent places for traineeship.<br>- Develop your own product concepts, prepare a portfolio and make it known through the Internet. Send it for competitions, etc.<br>- Look for a traineeship position in a marketing agency. |
| Sports and Physical education | Schools, clubs, sport teams, gyms, etc. | - Besides schools, clubs and gyms you can also look for opportunities in orphanages, nursing homes, prisons, etc.<br>- What about starting a walking morning group in your neighborhood? Or maybe a soccer, basketball, etc. team with your neighborhood children! |

| Law:<br>lawyer,<br>criminologist,<br>etc. | Law firms, police stations, detective offices, companies' legal departments, courthouses, etc. | - Most law offices are open for trainees.<br>- Offer your legal expertises to help non-governmental organizations, clubs, etc.<br>- Find out about opportunities to do a traineeship in a company's legal department. |
|---|---|---|
| Administratio n, Accounting and Economics | Basically every business needs the skills of such professionals. Financial institutions, such as banks, brokers, etc., are outstanding places for traineeships. | - Try to get an intern position in a company of a relative or a friend.<br>- Many clubs, associations, etc. don't have enough many to pay for a full-time accountant or economist; offer yourself to work as a volunteer.<br>- Your town administration office can be an excellent place to learn about public administration. |
| Pedagogy | Schools, orphanages, community associations, etc. | - Most schools are open for interns.<br>- Offer yourself to help in an orphanage.<br>- Join an educational project to help poor communities in your area or elsewhere.<br>- Prisons can be excellent places to introduce an educational project. |
| Engineering | Engineering companies, industries, labs, consulting companies, etc. | - Contact directly any company that deals with engineering projects, ask if they offer internship opportunities. If you know anyone in such a company, |

| | | |
|---|---|---|
| | | contact the person first and inquire about such opportunities.<br>- Some universities have groups called "Junior enterprise", where students can join industrial projects as consultants, get informed. If your university doesn't have one, start it.<br> More info at:<br>http://en.wikipedia.org/wiki/Junior_enterprise<br>www.jadenet.org<br>- Some banks have a department, where engineers review project applications for investment. Try to get an intern position in such a department. |
| Physics | Research institutes, schools, universities, companies that develop electro or electronic equipments, or optical instruments, etc. | - Schools are usually open for interns to help teaching physics.<br>- Companies that develop electro, electronic or optical instruments are excellent places for an internship.<br>- Power stations (hydro, nuclear, etc.) are also very good places for internship.<br>- Look for opportunities in astronomy or meteorology laboratories. |
| Geography | Schools, universities, public transport | - Apply for an intern position at the public transport department of your city. |

| | department, companies that develop maps, etc. | - Look for some areas of your city that were not yet well studied and write a paper about it and submit for your local newspaper or a scientific journal.<br>- Apply for a traineeship in a company that offers ecotourism. |
|---|---|---|
| Geology | Mining and oil companies, engineering companies, archeology labs, museums, etc. | - Develop your research and publishing skills. Draw a geological map of an unknown area of your city.<br>- Some banks have departments to analyze the environment impact of projects, try to join them.<br>- Environment agencies are excellent places for an internship.<br>- Civil engineering companies are also open for internship opportunities. |
| History | Schools, museums, universities, archives, etc. | - Do a research about an interesting event that took place in your city, organize a good material, write an article and submit it to your local newspaper or write a booklet and publish it.<br>- Try to become an intern in a museum, archive or in an office that works restoring old documents.<br>- What about researching your own family's genealogy tree? |

| | | |
|---|---|---|
| | | It could potentially become an interesting book.<br>- Prepare a historical tour guide for your city and present your material to the tourism department.<br>- Movie and documentary producers usually need a historian's help for their work. Contact them.<br>- What about a book or a video on the history of your local church, sport club, etc. or still the biography of an interesting character of your city? |
| Languages: interpreter, translator, teacher, etc. | Translation companies, schools, export departments, tourism agencies, hotels, newspapers, embassies and consulates, etc. | - Visiting a museum or an art gallery is usually a pleasure, but it can be frustrating, when we don't understand what the things are about, because the descriptions are only written in a local language. Thus offer your services to translate the texts from the local languages to others you are proficient. The same can be done for a Zoo. Guests from other countries will be very thankful.<br>- If you live in a touristic city, offer your translation skills for tourists. Prepare a business card and distribute in hotels and touristic centers.<br>- Distribute your business |

| | | card in police stations, they may need you services.<br>- Try to get a job at an airport, central station, conference center, etc. |
| Informatics: computer science, programming, etc. | There are plenty of opportunities in small companies as well as in big corporations. | - Offer your services to implement a computer system in a friend's company or any institution such as a local school, clubs, etc.<br>- You can also voluntarily teach in a school, orphanage, prison, etc. |
| Journalism | Radio and TV stations, newspapers, magazines, marketing agencies, political parties, etc. | - Obviously you should first of all try to work as an trainee in a radio or TV station or in a local newspaper.<br>- Start a blog about something you like to write about. Many people do that already, therefore you must invest in quality and differentiation.<br>- Big companies usually have a public relations department. Try to join one as a trainee.<br>- Politicians usually need press agents.<br>- Organize a local newspaper for you district, school, university, etc.<br>- Prepare a documentary about something interesting that happened your city, school, etc. and publish in the Internet for example.<br>- Become a freelance journalist |

| | | and start writing for newspapers, blogs, etc. |
|---|---|---|
| Mathematics, Statistics, etc. | Banks, investment companies, clinical trial companies, computer science labs, schools, opinion poll companies, etc. | - Banks and investment companies need professionals with solid knowledge of mathematics. Get informed!<br>- Research companies and laboratories usually need professionals to help with statistics. |
| Meteorology | Airports, agriculture agencies, weather related companies. | - Get informed about the possibility to start as trainee in an local agriculture agency.<br>- Airports and weather related companies are excellent places for an internship. |
| Medicine, nursing, physiotherapy, psychology, etc. | Hospitals, clinics, orphanages, nursing homes, prisons, etc. | - This is probably one of the easiest areas to find an internship position. Hospitals, clinics, etc. are usually open for trainees and volunteers.<br>- Get involved with any non-profit organization that offers medical services, for example: Red Cross, ADRA, Doctors Without Borders, etc.<br>- Churches often need professionals from the medical field to join their mission trips and projects. Get informed! |
| Chemistry | Chemical and pharmaceutical companies, water treatment and recycling | - Basically any materials processing company can be potentially interesting for a chemist.<br>- Together with you |

| | | |
|---|---|---|
| | companies, as well as food and cosmetic industries, etc. | classmates start a "Junior Enterprise" in the field of chemistry.<br>- Try to get an intern position at the company that does the wastewater treatment for your city. |
| Philosophy, Sociology, etc. | Governmental offices, political parties, opinion poll companies, newspapers, non-governmental organizations, etc. | - Apply for an intern position in a political party.<br>- Get involved with public opinion researches.<br>- Do your own research about any peculiar local group (punks, hippies, etc.), write an article about it and publish it.<br>- Publish your own ideas. Write articles to the local newspapers, your own blog, etc. |
| Theology | Churches, armed forces, orphanages, hospitals, publishing houses, etc. | - Offer your services to help the leader of your local church.<br>- Hospitals, prisons, and orphanages are excellent places to exercise your theological skills.<br>- You can use your knowledge to help museums, history or philosophy groups, as well as religious publishing houses, etc. |
| Tourism | Hotels, tourism agencies and companies, publishing houses, etc. | - Try to get an intern position in your local tourism agency.<br>- If your city doesn't have a department of tourism, then prepare a report showing the |

| | | tourism potential of your city. Submit the report to the Major of your city or publish in the local newspaper. |
| | | - Become intern in a hotel.<br>- Start your own blog about tourism in your city, or even in your district. Describe about historical places, new ways, etc. |

# Acknowledgments

I would like to thank Joseph for the excellent examples he left, Moses for writing everything and obviously God for inspiring both of the them.

My wife deserves more than my gratitude for being so patient with me, while I spent so much time working on this book.

I must also thank my reviewers who were so patient and talented in reading and fixing my first writings and turning this work into a enjoyable book: Miriam, Pompílio, Thomas Lopes, Almir, Dulce, Alano, Evandro, Steven, Stephanie and my uncle Eugênio.

Many thanks to the following brilliant people who were so kind to help me with the English version: Roderich (Rodrigo), Maria Jimenez, Carol van der Zee, Cristina Almeida, Catrin Warning and Pastor Milton.

Thank you Roberto for the excellent design work and for the valuable discussions.

To my interviewees: Dimpy, Rokas, Bill, Almir, Erwin, Ruben, Agnus, Dulce and Don.

I must also thank all those who directly or indirectly helped me with ideas: Ausra, Maria (my mother), Almir, Elio, Siara, Yvonne, Edson, Vieira, Thomas Freier, Casten, Veit Otto, Nina, Tina, Susanne, Michael, Alano, Werber, and all my friends from the SDA churches in Darmstadt, Berlin and Toronto.

# References

## Chapter 1


1 - Kim, Karl H. S., Relkin, Norman R., Lee, Kyoung-Min and Hirsch, Joy; Distinct cortical areas associated with native and second languages. Nature 388(July 10):171, (1997)
2 - http://discovermagazine.com/1997/oct/ thebilingualbrai1258
3 - www.lankanewspapers.com/news/2008/3/ 25617_space.html
4 - Smollins, John-Pierre, "The Making of the History: Ninety Years of Northeastern Co-op", Northeastern University Magazine 24 (5), May, (1999) http://www.northeastern.edu/magazine/9905/history.html
5 - http://en.wikipedia.org/wiki/Cooperative_ education#CITEREFSmollins1999
6 - http://en.wikipedia.org/wiki/Cooperative_education
7 - http://www.cecs.uwaterloo.ca/


## Chapter 2


1 - Navarro, Joe and Kerlins, Marvin; "What every BODY is saying", Corlins Living, United States of America, (2008)
2 - Reiman,Tonya; The Power of Body Language, Pocket Books, (2007)
3 - Cohen, David; Body Language, What you need to know, (2007)
4- Argyle, M.; Bodily communication (2nd edition). New York: International Universities Press. (1990)
5 - http://cogprints.org/4444/1/Body_Language_ is_Important_ in_Large_Groups.pdf
6 - http://personal-development101.blogspot.com/2008/12/body-language-louder-than-words.html
7 - http://www.best-job-interview.com/interview-body-language.html
8 - http://www.humanresourcesiq.com/sponsor_article.cfm? externalID=3072

9 - http://en.wikipedia.org/wiki/Body_language

10 - http://www.bodylanguagetips.com/body-language-secrets

11 - http://www.slideshare.net/aidenyeh/nonverbal-communication

12 - http://talkbank.org/media/PDF/JOC-PDF/2-Buck20%26%20VanLear.pdf

13 - Mehrabian, Albert and Wiener, Morton; Decoding of inconsistent communications. Journal of personality and social psychology 6(1): 109-114, (1991)

14 - http://www.ecademy.com/node.php?id=78144

15 - http://en.wikipedia.org/wiki/Body_language

16 - Byrne, John; CEO Disease, Business Week, 1 April, 52-59, (1991)

17 - Goleman, Daniel, Boyatzis, Richard and Mckee, Annie; The new leaders; Harvard Business School Press, United States of America, (2002)

18 - Conway, James and Huffcutt, Allen; "Psychometric properties of Multi-source     Performance Ratings: A Meta-analysis of Subordinate, Supervisor, Peer and Self-Ratings" Human Performance 10, no. 4: 331-360, (1977)

19 - Stuart, Peggy; "What Does the Glass Ceiling Cost You?" Personal Journal 71, no. 11: 70-80, (1992)

20 - Morrison, Ann M., White, Randall P. and Van Velsor, Ellen; The Center for Creative Leadership: Can Women Reach the Top of America's Largest Corporations? Reading, MA: Addison-Wesley, (1987)

21 - Cox Jr., Taylor; Cultural Diversity in Organizations: Theory, Research, and Practise San Francisco: Berret-Koehler Publishers, (1993)

22 - http://cogprints.org/4444/1/Body_Language_is_ Important_in_ Large_Groups.pdf

23 - Rollman, Steven A.; The Journal of Social Psycology, 105, 73-77, (1978)

24 - Dickey, E. C., Knower, F. H.; A note on some ethnological differences in recognition of simulated expression of emotions. Amer. J. Sociol., 47, 190-193 (1941)

## Chapter 3

1 - Granovetter, Mark, Getting a Job, Chicago: University of Chicago Press (1995)
2 - Gladwell, Malcolm, The Tipping Point, Abacus, 2008.
3 - Hill, Brian E. and Dee Power, Inside Secrets to Venture Capital, John Wiley & Sons, Inc. Canada (2001)

## Chapter 4

1 - http://sbinfocanada.about.com/
2 - http://sbinfocanada.about.com/cs/management/qt/telephonetips.htm
3 - Goleman, Daniel, Boyatzis, Richard and Mckee, Annie; The New Leaders; Harvard Business School Press, United States of America (2002)

## Chapter 5

1 - http://www.toronto-bia.com/index.php?
option=com_content&task=view&id=113&Itemid=1
2 - http://www.fao.org/inpho/content/ compend/text/ch23_03.htm
3 - http://nobelprize.org/nobel_prizes/peace/ laureates/2006/press.htm
4 - Marquis, Christopher and Battilana, Julie; Acting Globally but Thinking Locally? The Influence of Local Communities on Organizations, Havard business school, Nov. (2007)
http://hbswk.hbs.edu/item/5823.html
5 - http://consumer-responsibility.suite101.com/
article.cfm/supporting_the_local_small_business_owner

## Chapter 6

1 - House (also known as House, M.D.) is an American television medical drama created by David Shore. The show's central character is Dr. Gregory House (Hugh Laurie).
http://en.wikipedia.org/wiki/House_(TV_series)
2 - Feldman, Robert; The Liar in Your Life: The Way to Truthful Relationships, Ed. Twelve (2009)
3 - Lodi, João Bosco; A entrevista, teoria e prática. Sétima edição. Biblioteca pioneira de administração e negócios, São Paulo (1991)
4 - Camp, Jim; Start with NO...The Negotiating Tools that the Pros Don't Want You to Know. Crown Business New York (2002)


## Chapter 7

1 - Jennings, William E.; Entrepreneurship: A Primer for Canadians. Toronto: Canadian Foundation for Economic Education (1985)
http://sbinfocanada.about.com/cs/startup/a/startownbiz_2.htm
2 - http://www.growthink.com/content/7-entrepreneurs-whose-perseverance-will-inspire-you
3 - Mullins, John, Komissar, Randy; Getting to plan B, Harvard Business Press, Boston (2009)
4 - http://www.high-tech-gruenderfonds.de/
5 - www.aspiras.de
6 - Covey, Stephen R.; The 7 habits of highly effective people, Fireside, New York (1989)
7 - White, Ellen; Temperança. http://www.ellenwhitebooks.com/
8 - Goleman, Daniel, Boyatzis, Richard, Mckee, Annie; The New Leaders; Harvard Business School Press, United States of America (2002)

**To obtain more copies of this book
or a version in a different
language, please access:**


**www.josephceo.com**